THE COMPLETE GUIDE TO
Hypnosis

*the text of this book is printed
on 100% recycled paper*

THE COMPLETE GUIDE TO
Hypnosis

by
Leslie M. LeCron

BARNES & NOBLE BOOKS

A DIVISION OF HARPER & ROW, PUBLISHERS

New York, Hagerstown, San Francisco, London

A hardcover edition of this book is published by Nash Publishing.

First BARNES & NOBLE BOOKS edition published 1973.

STANDARD BOOK NUMBER: 06-463361-6

80 12 11

Contents

THE COMPLETE GUIDE TO
Hypnosis

Introduction

In recent years there have been many books published on the subject of hypnosis, but most were texts for the professional practitioner. This book is intended to provide full information for anyone who wishes to learn more about hypnosis and to obtain the facts about it. It should counteract popular misconceptions which have caused some people to fear hypnosis, and which have given it an aspect of mystery and magic. With proper understanding and knowledge about hypnosis, its benefits can become more readily available to many others.

It is doubtful that at the end of World War II there were even as many as two hundred professional men — physicians, psychologists, and dentists — who used hypnosis in their practices. Today there are probably almost twenty thousand, although no statistics are available. As professional interest has increased, so popular interest has also developed. Hundreds of thousands of persons have experienced hypnosis. Their telling has led many more to become interested in this fascinating subject.

During the past few years, since hypnosis has become an acceptable tool in professional use, much more has been learned about it, although our knowledge is still far from adequate. Where money for research in hypnosis was formerly almost impossible to obtain (investigators might as well have asked for money for research in witchcraft), now the U.S. Department of Public Health, as well as many foundations, has made grants for research. Many individuals and a few psychology departments in universities have obtained funds and carried out research.

There are now three professional organizations devoted to hypnosis, each of them issuing quarterly journals which publish the results of research, and still other scientific papers about hypnosis. The Society for Clinical and Experimental Hypnosis was the first of these societies to be formed (in 1949). Its address is 353 W. 57th St., New York, N.Y., 10019. The other two societies are the American Society for Clinical Hypnosis, 800 Washington Ave. Southeast, Minneapolis, Minn. 55414, the largest in membership, and the American Society of Psychosomatic Dentistry and Medicine, 2802 Mermaid Ave., Brooklyn, N.Y. 11224. Anyone may subscribe to the journals which they publish. Membership in all three is restricted to qualified physicians, psychologists, and dentists.

I have tried in the following pages to show not only how hypnosis can be used by its practitioners but also how the individual himself can use it to advantage — self-hypnosis.

I believe the reader will find most interesting the method given for obtaining information from the subconscious part of the mind by means of unconsciously controlled signals in response to questions. Technically, this is by ideomotor movement. This technique proves that the inner part of the mind thinks and reasons, a fact which many are not aware of. It provides a means of direct communication with that part of our mental makeup. The technique has been taught to several thousand practitioners who have taken the courses given by Hypnosis Symposiums, a group giving such classes and of which I am one of the instructors.

LESLIE M. LE CRON
Rt. 2, Box 1388
Carmel, Cal. 93921

1
What Is Hypnosis?

Just what is hypnosis? That is a very difficult question to answer. While we know a good deal about hypnosis, there is still much which we do not know. We can describe it, but no one has yet come up with a theory which will fit in every respect. One part of the difficulty is that there is such a great difference between a light state of hypnosis and a deep one.

It may surprise you to know that you've been self-hypnotized spontaneously hundreds or even thousands of times. Although these spontaneous states are not ordinarily termed hypnosis, that is just what they are. These spontaneous states occur probably every day of our lives. Do you ever day-dream? Everyone does. It's a state of hypnosis. When you become absorbed in anything — reading a book, in your work, in a hobby — you slip into hypnosis. There are many other situations where self-hypnosis develops spontaneously — an interesting lecture, motion picture, television program, or religious ceremony can bring on self-hypnosis.

4

Have you ever watched a TV program with young people dancing to rock and roll music? If you will notice the dancers, most of them are in hypnosis. There is a complete lack of expression on their faces and they do not speak. This is not too surprising if it is realized that priests and witch doctors of all primitive races use hypnosis and induce it with rhythm — chanting, dancing, and music, particularly with drum beats. These are all conducive to hypnosis.

Almost anyone who has not experienced hypnosis or who has not read a book about it or heard someone talk about it will have many misconceptions, and may fear being hypnotized. It is really rather strange that these common misconceptions or ideas persist when modern hypnosis has been known for some two hundred years.

The most common mistaken idea is that a hypnotized person will pass out and be unconscious. This never happens, even in the very deepest stages. There is always awareness. People often believe they will be in the power of the hypnotist and would have to do anything they were told to do. Willpower is not lost. No one will do anything in hypnosis which is contrary to his moral code. This obviously is true, or there would be frequent bad reports of things done by hypnotized subjects. It is not hard to learn how to hypnotize, and there are many unscrupulous people in this world. They would certainly find hypnosis most helpful if people could be put under their control. Suggestions given to a subject are censored both consciously and subconsciously, and will be carried out only if they are acceptable.

A subject will sometimes ask the operator, "What would happen if you died while I was hypnotized?" or "What if you could not awaken me?" It is a very rare matter for anyone to fail to come out of hypnosis when told to do so. It can happen, but a professional who has hypnotized thousands of persons may never have had this occur. Actually there is no danger in such a situation, and the professional operator knows how to handle it. This will be discussed more at length in the chapter about the so-called "dangers." As a matter of fact, if nothing at all was done the subject would awaken after a time. Anyone in hypnosis can awaken himself at any time he might wish to do so.

Sometimes a person is afraid he might talk while in hypnosis and give away some "state secret," something he would not want known. Since there is always complete awareness, naturally, no subject will ever expose anything of this nature. He knows just what he is saying or doing.

A person may say, "I don't think I'll be a good subject because I have a strong mind." Actually it is the strongminded person of good intelligence who makes the best subject. In general it can be said that the higher a person's IQ, the better a subject he will be. Of course there are many exceptions to this very broad statement, for other things can act to prevent a genius from being hypnotized.

As to the question of what a person experiences when hypnotized, this will vary considerably with the individual and depend on the depth which is reached. There is very little sensation felt in a light or even medium state – a listlessness or lethargy is present. The subject feels as if he can move, speak, or open his eyes, and he can. However, it also seems too troublesome, and subjects will seldom bother to if even in only a light state of hypnosis.

The idea of passing out seems to be so well-established with many that they cannot believe they were hypnotized when actually they were. Most operators tell the subject initially that he will be aware, but after being awakened it is not uncommon for the subject to say, "Well, that's too bad. I guess it didn't work, for I heard everything you said." It is perhaps unfortunate that something does not "click" in the mind, or that there is not more actual sensation — particularly in the lighter stage of hypnosis.

Some subjects will recall that they felt very heavy, especially in their arms and legs. Others have had almost the opposite effect, and felt very light as if they were floating.

While there is always awareness, the operator is dealing to a greater extent with the subconscious mind of the subject. The subject's thoughts are bubbling up mostly from the inner mind, which can be much more readily influenced. The inner mind thinks and reasons, although in a somewhat different way than the conscious mind. This can readily be demonstrated, and will be discussed later.

Most operators try to show the hypnotized subject that something is different, realizing that he probably is wondering if he is hypnotized. Sometimes a test is made which convinces the subject. Sometimes some hypnotic phenomenon is suggested, such as anesthesia of one hand, or some other convincing phenomenon.

In a deep trance (hypnosis is definitely a trance state) there is much more awareness of being hypnotized. Thought processes are slower. The lethargy is greater. If asked to speak, the subject finds talking difficult at first, which is probably due to the lethargy. Sometimes he can be brought out of hypnosis with a complete amnesia for all that happened while he was hypnotized.

Several theories have been formulated about hypnosis. As stated, none really fits completely. We can describe hypnosis but cannot define it in all its aspects. It is a somewhat altered state of consciousness and altered awareness, although the conscious mind is still present. We might compare it to a teeter-totter. In the waking state the conscious mind is at the high end of the teeter-totter and the subconscious mind at the low end. Under hypnosis they reverse and the subconscious is at the high end and the conscious part at the low end, but it is still present. Thoughts rise from the inner mind into consciousness.

Another pronounced attribute of hypnosis is that suggestibility is greatly increased. In a deep state a subject may carry out suggested acts which are quite ridiculous, as seen in stage hypnotism performances. Suggestions, like emotions, can even cause physical bodily changes, and affect the action of organs and glands.

Another attribute of hypnosis, greater in the deeper stages, is called *rapport*. The subject seems to want to do whatever is suggested to him, provided it is not something contrary to his moral code. He feels a close relationship to the hypnotist. It has been said that rapport was so strong the hypnotized subject would respond only to the person who had hypnotized him and no one else. This saying is sometimes true but it seems to depend entirely on the attitude of the subject. He may find it too much trouble to respond to someone else, but usually will do so. If he does not, and is questioned afterwards and asked if he heard the voice of the other person talking to him, he will probably say he heard him but it was too much trouble to answer and he didn't want to be bothered.

One theory about hypnosis was held by some of the old-timers such as Liebeault and Bernheim, and advanced by the great Pavlov. This was the principle that hypnosis is a form of sleep. A hypnotized person whose eyes are closed certainly looks as if he is asleep, and the lethargy displayed also indicates it. Of course this theory does not hold because there is always awareness while the subject is in hypnosis. Also, the sleep pattern shown with encephalography is not present, nor is the patelar reflex (the knee jerk when the knee is tapped). This is present when one is awake, but lost during sleep.

A theory advanced by a psychiatrist named Ferenczi and known as the psychoanalytic theory is that the hypnotized person accepts the hypnotist as a substitute parent and then regresses and becomes infantile. Anyone who has been hypnotized will refute this theory as being far-fetched and untrue.

Another theory holds that hypnosis is a conditioned reflex developed in the course of maturing from words, etc., that are a part of past experiences.

One theory held by several competent authorities is that a hypnotized person will behave as he thinks a hypnotized person should behave. This implies that hypnosis is entirely artificial. It would seem that this is partly true in lighter stages and is related to the rapport phenomenon. Another aspect of this theory is that all hypnotic phenomena can at times be produced by subjects not in hypnosis. However, this theory is completely refuted by several facts. It doesn't explain how a person can be hypnotized by an indirect method and then be completely unaware that he is hypnotized. Another refutation is that young children can be deeply hypnotized and of course have not the slightest knowledge of how a hypnotized person should behave. It also tends to ignore self-hypnosis.

Perhaps the most satisfactory theory, but still one that doesn't meet all considerations, is that of dissociation. This theory was embraced by Janet and many other earlier authorities but today is favored by few. The normal act of recalling memories is a result of the association of ideas. Dissociation is the failure of the power to recall things which normally should be remembered — an interruption or repression of memory. Amnesia is therefore an essential element in the theory. The dissociation theory is largely based on the fact of spontaneous amnesia following a deep state of hypnosis, but there certainly is little dissociation, if any, in a light stage. The inner part of the mind never forgets, not even the slightest detail of what happens to us.

Some other ideas have also been advanced, such as theories based on changes in brain physiology, or that hypnosis is due to electromagnetic fields involving cortical areas.

Scientists of any persuasion like to have theories to work with, but at present we can only describe hypnosis rather than to theorize correctly about it.

2
The Background of Hypnosis

Hypnosis has been used through history by priests, witch doctors, and healers. The oldest reference is found in the Evers papyrus of three thousand years ago, in Egypt. The ancient Greeks had sleep temples where patients came to be healed and were put into hypnosis. All primitive races have used hypnosis and do so at present.

The modern history of hypnosis usually is considered as beginning with Franz Anton Mesmer, a physician who originally practiced in Vienna and later moved to Paris when his colleagues persecuted him. He developed the theory that the body has a magnetic polarity with a force field, which he termed *animal magnetism*. He thought this was developed in everyone in varying degree, but that certain gifted persons could exert it most forcefully.

11

Mesmer had good success with his treatments of patients in Vienna, but did even better in Paris. At this period, the late eighteenth century, there was no form of psychotherapy available. Those who suffered from neuroses, psychosomatic illnesses, or character disturbances could receive no treatment other than simple reassurance. Mesmer's methods were successful, although he undoubtedly also had failures. He became the vogue with the French nobility and upper classes, and his practice was most profitable financially. Of course this earned him the enmity of his colleagues.

Mesmer asked the French Academy of Science to investigate his methods, but was then refused. Such an investigation was made later by Benjamin Franklin, the U.S. Ambassador to France, who was on the committee appointed for this purpose. Miffed, Mesmer would not cooperate and only his followers were the objects of the investigation. The committee, ignoring the fact that Mesmer did have good results, reported adversely, claiming results came only from imagination. This discredited Mesmer, who finally returned to Austria and died in obscurity.

The term *mesmerism,* or animal magnetism, was adopted for his methods and his followers persisted in its use. The Marquis de Puysegur had a very good subject in a peasant lad named Victor Race, who diagnosed illnesses while under hypnosis — something along the lines of the famous psychic Edgar Cayce in the twentieth century.

The history of hypnosis has been a series of periods of great interest followed by the persecution of its advocates, with a resulting decline in interest. Following the discrediting of Mesmer, there was such a lull until the period between 1820 to 1830. Interest again arose in the 1840's, particularly in England. There, one of the greatest surgeons, John Elliotson, became interested in animal magnetism. It was he who first introduced the use of the stethescope in England. He performed many operations with only hypnotic anesthesia, for drug anesthetics were not yet known. He was condemned by his colleagues for his use of hypnosis and was asked to resign from his position as head of the staff at the University of London hospital. In spite of persecution, Elliotson refused to give up his use of hypnosis, citing its use as being of too great value.

Another British surgeon, James Esdaile, working in a prison hospital in India during the 1840's, saw a demonstration of mesmerism in England while on vacation. He witnessed anesthesia induced in a hypnotized subject. Returning to India, he began to use the methods he had seen demonstrated. Esdaile performed over three thousand operations with hypnosis as the sole anesthetic agent, over three hundred being major surgeries. One observer told of witnessing Esdaile remove a cancerous eye from a patient while the other eye look on unblinkingly.

Like others, Esdaile was persecuted by his colleagues. He was forced to close his hospital in India and returned to England, where the British Medical Association tried him for charlatanism. During the trial one physician claimed that Esdaile was sacrilegious, because God meant for man to feel pain and Esdaile was preventing this with hypnosis.

Another British physician of that era, James Braid, decided that the induction method of the mesmerists produced hypnosis only because the subject expected this to happen. Actually, it was suggestion that caused the trance. The mesmeric method was to make passes over the patient's body, thus supposedly transmitting the animal magnetic fluid through the operator's hands and into the subject to produce the trance. Braid tried inductions through only verbal suggestion, at the same time using eye fixation by the subject. He found this quite successful and coined the words *hypnotism* and *hypnosis* from the Greek work for sleep, *hypnos.*

Interest, again waning, was revived around 1880, when one of the leading French physicians, Bernheim, became interested and joined in practice with Liebeault, a country doctor practicing in Nancy and devoting himself to hypnosis. He had adopted Braid's ideas of induction through suggestion. The work of these two men was so successful that physicians including Sigmund Freud, the developer of psychoanalytic methods, came from all over Europe and America to learn their methods. This period was probably the heyday of hypnosis prior to the present time.

With the turn of the century interest again waned, largely due to the fact that Freud had originally used hypnosis and then abandoned it. His followers, even today, have taken the attitude that because Freud tried hypnosis and found it useless, it is of no value. This is the current attitude of most psychoanalysts and many psychiatrists trained in Freudian methods. On the other hand, hundreds of psychiatrists do use hypnosis and find it of the utmost value.

Freud was really a very poor hypnotist while his colleague of that period, Breuer, was one of the leading medical hypnotists. Freud could not tolerate Breuer's success as compared to his own failures. Also, Freud had the mistaken idea that a deep trance was necessary in order to use hypnosis successfully, and he could only obtain a deep state with a small number of his patients. He knew nothing of modern techniques in hypnotherapy. He was also greatly embarrassed one day when a woman patient in hypnosis threw her arms around him just as someone came into the room.

Following World War I there was some interest again in hypnosis since it was used successfully for the treatment of battle fatigue, offering a shortcut in treatment. The first use along analytic lines by seeking causes for conditions was by Hadfield, a British psychiatrist.

Modern interest began after World War II, when hypnosis again had been found of great advantage in the treatment of the neuroses which developed from battle. It is very doubtful that in 1945 there were even as many as two hundred professional men in the United States who used hypnosis. Today there are probably twenty thousand who have had courses in the techniques of hypnosis, most of them utilizing it in their work.

In 1955, a committee appointed by the British Medical Association reported that hypnosis was a valuable tool in medical treatment. The association then urged that it be taught in the medical schools and gave its approval for physicians to learn its use. This was the first time orthodox medical approval had ever been given to hypnosis. In 1958 the American Medical Association followed suit after a similar committee had investigated and reported favorably. While hypnosis still has some stigma attached to it by some physicians, its advocates no longer are subject to professional persecution because of it.

Despite the recommendations of these societies, very few medical or dental schools have offered courses in hypnosis. Most of the courses available to physicians, psychologists, and dentists have been those given by groups of individuals privately. Hypnosis Symposiums, of which I am an instructor, has given ninety-six such courses since 1954. These have been offered in all parts of the United States, in Canada, Mexico, Jamaica, and Puerto Rico. Several other groups have also offered courses following the success of Hypnosis Symposiums, and the professional societies now give "workshop" classes in connection with their annual conventions.

With the official acceptance of hypnosis and the findings of its value in medical and dental treatments and in psychotherapy, it is probable that interest will be maintained instead of being lost again. The present time sees much scientific research being conducted — some in schools and by organizations, and much more by individuals.

3
The Phenomena of Hypnosis

With only one exception, all of the phenomena which can be induced in the hypnotic subject were known to the old-time mesmerists. The one exception is the distortion of time, which will be considered later in this chapter. The first use of hypnotic anesthesia was for a tooth extraction, in 1821. Two years later, in 1823, it was first used for childbirth.

As already mentioned, one of the attributes or phenomena of hypnosis is the greatly increased *suggestibility* which develops spontaneously. Children are very suggestible and are usually the best hypnotic subjects. Suggestibility and hypnotizability go hand in hand and are almost the same. There is also greatly increased suggestibility when a person is emotional, and it is quite likely that one then enters spontaneously into self-hypnosis without realizing it.

A *post-hypnotic suggestion* is one given while a person is hypnotized but which is to be carried out afterwards, usually while he is awake. Sometimes a subject may spontaneously slip back into hypnosis while carrying out such a suggestion, awakening again when this is completed. Being able to implant beneficial suggestions to be carried out later can be a valuable procedure.

Subjects will carry out a very bizarre post-hypnotic suggestion sometimes and, when questioned as to why they did something quite unusual, will rationalize their behavior. One evening when some physician friends were present, I was giving a demonstration with a young married woman acting as a subject. I gave her the post-hypnotic suggestion that she would remove one of her shoes after she had awakened and would place it on the table in front of her. She was told she would not remember having been given this suggestion.

After she had awakened, she fidgeted for a few moments, then slipped off one of her shoes with the other foot, reached down, lifted it, and placed it on the table in front of her. Then she reached over and took the flowers from a vase on the table and placed them in her shoe. This was unexpected and I asked why she had done this. "Oh," she explained, "I have a vase at home that looks something like a shoe. I wondered what kind of flower arrangement I could use with it." Not remembering the suggestion given her, she needed to rationalize her action, in order to have some reason for carrying out such a nonsensical procedure.

A subject usually seems to develop an attitude toward the person who has hypnotized him; this is termed *rapport*. He wants to please the operator and be cooperative, although sometimes there are reasons for resistance. Rapport may bring a kind of role-playing on the part of the subject. This phenomenon is of great advantage for both patient and operator during hypnotherapy.

One interesting phenomenon is called *catalepsy*. By definition catalepsy is a change in muscular tonus, which may be either extreme rigidity of a group of muscles, such as a limb, or the opposite, great flaccidity. It also involves a tendency for a limb to remain in any position in which it is placed, even an awkward, uncomfortable one. In this case there seems to be no discomfort felt. There may be, similarly, an inability to lift a limb or move it, maybe because it is too much effort or because it seems too heavy.

Stage hypnotists often demonstrate catalepsy in a very dramatic way. The subject on the stage is given suggestions for his entire body to become completely cataleptic: stiff and rigid. He is then placed across two chairs, his head on one and his feet on the other, lying stiffly. The hypnotist will then sit, or even stand, on the subject's midsection while rigidity is maintained even with this weight on him, and apparently with no effort. This is obviously something that might prove highly dangerous. There is no way of telling the subject's physical condition and he certainly could be injured in this way. What if he had a hernia? No professional man would ever demonstrate in this way!

While under hypnosis there seems to be much greater ability to remember, to be able to recall past experiences or forgotton memories of other kinds. This is called *hypermnesia*. In more common language it is simply better memory recall.

One of the most interesting of all hypnotic phenomena is *age regression*, which is somewhat related to hypermnesia. There is no doubt that the subconscious part of the mind registers in the memory department everything that happens to us, and stores even the slightest detail. Consciously we can only draw on a very small part of our total memory. With hypnosis and age regression it is possible to cause a subject to go back in time and to relive previous events. While memory is involved, this is much more than merely remembering. Seemingly, it is a reliving with all five senses acting. The regressed person sees, hears, feels, and if smell and taste were involved, they are also re-experienced. If questioned, he will say it seemed as if the event were actually happening again.

There are two forms of age regression. One is apparently total, or seems so. It has been termed revivification. A deep stage is required in order to produce it. With this form the subject seems to become the suggested age. If told he is five years old he behaves as a five-year-old child would and blots out everything in time after that age. If asked to write something, he probably would only print, which most children learn at about that age. Psychological tests given at different age levels to regressed subjects bear out that these regressions are actual, though not always completely so.

Much easier to produce is a different type of regression which might be termed partial. This only requires a light state of hypnosis and is usually very easily developed. Again, it is reliving rather than merely remembering. However, the subject seems conscious of his present situation as well, there being a kind of duality present. He can talk to the operator and he will be aware of the operator's identity and of his own special location. With the complete type, the operator is an anachronism, for the subject did not know him at the regressed age. With the complete type of regression, if a subject is taken to an early age, before speech was learned, he is unable to talk. With the partial type of regression he can talk readily and tell what is happening.

This partial form of regression is very valuable in hypnotherapy. It is also helpful in uncovering and removing any blocks which may be affecting a student's ability to learn or to study.

Sometimes an experience in the past is too traumatic to be brought into consciousness. It is too frightening or emotional to be tolerated at a conscious level. Here an expedient is possible. Instead of having the person go through this experience, regressing to it, he is told under hypnosis to go back to it but to see it as an observer instead of as the participant. This takes much of the fear or other emotions away. The subject is able to see and hear what happens, but can now depersonalize it. After reviewing the event three or four times as an observer, it may be quite safe to regress to it as the participant. This can be determined from the answers given with the questioning technique, which is explained later.

To what age is it possible to regress a subject? This brings up the question as to when memory actually begins. Is it at birth or even before? or at one, two, or three years old? Few people can remember much that happened to them before about five years of age, though there may be a very few earlier memories. Almost no one can consciously remember happenings before three years old. With hypnotic regression a subject can even be taken back to his birth. Some think this is only fantasy, but many hypnotherapists are convinced that such a regression is factual and that there is a definite memory in the subconscious mind of the birth experience.

Can hypnotic age regression be produced during self-hypnosis? Some have been able to do so; others could not. It may be impossible to self-regress to a traumatic or frightening event, particularly if it has been repressed, but sometimes it can be done. More likely will be the recall of an experience instead of reliving it.

A young woman who had learned self-hypnosis was unable to afford psychotherapy, but decided to see what she could do herself to be rid of asthma attacks. She had been a psychiatric social worker and sometimes had to enter a hospital in her work. This always brought on strong fear reactions which she recognized as phobic. Another phobia was the sight of the bare, hairy arms of a man. Still another involved knives. As a child she would run from the dining table when her father carved. Other than these symptoms she was well-adjusted, happy, in good health, and competent in her work. She had read much about psychotherapy and about hypnosis.

Part of Mrs. R.'s self-treatment with self-hypnosis was carried out in bed at night before going to sleep. One night while in hypnosis she determined to explore her childhood systematically. She began searching back in memory, starting at the age of fourteen. Her attempt was to recall anything pertinent, particularly traumatic experiences, because of a "feeling" that a traumatic episode might be involved.

Mrs. R. worked through a number of minor emotional events of childhood, but with the impression that they were unimportant. One completely forgotten incident at the age of five was recalled with unusual clarity. Then, very suddenly, she seemed to be lying on a table, clothed in a white gown, and under brilliant lights. She could see a man, also in white, standing beside her holding a small knife.

Above her head was a vague, threatening object which was coming down over her face. She was terrified and struggled to rise, but two hairy arms seized her and roughly forced her back on the table. She continued to struggle and was grasped violently and shaken, then a hand slapped her sharply and repeatedly. The object came down over her face, smothering her. At this point she began to scream, which awakened her husband. She was trembling and sobbing and he had difficulty quieting her.

The next day, Mrs. R. questioned her mother and learned that at the age of sixteen months a mastoidectomy had been performed on her. She had been very sick afterward with severe shock complications. Two of the hospital nurses had informed the mother of the brutality shown toward the child by the anesthetist and they had resigned in protest. For some time the child had experienced nightmares and been emotionally upset. Shortly after the operation her first attack of asthma had occurred.

Having brought this experience into consciousness with spontaneous age regression (although she had been trying to regress), she was subsequently free of asthma, and had lost both her phobias. She no longer was afraid of hairy arms or of knives, or afraid of being in a hospital.

This case does show that it is possible to regress with self-hypnosis, even to a very traumatic experience. Perhaps this was made possible by her knowledge of psychotherapy and of hypnosis, plus her determination to rid herself of her asthma and her phobias. She had become an excellent subject, and was very good with self-hypnosis.

Still another very valuable phenomenon is the ability to shut off the sensation of pain under hypnosis – *hypnotic anesthesia*. Thousands of women have gone through childbirth under hypnosis and have felt no pain or had partial anesthesia, minimizing the pain. Major surgery of various kinds has been performed with no anesthesia but hypnosis. This has included heart operations and limb amputations. This is usually done when there are contraindications for the use of drug anesthesia. For minor surgery and in dentistry, hypnotic anesthesia is rather easily produced.

With a good subject, *hallucinations* of any of the five senses can be suggested. They can be positive or negative in character. Often demonstrated is the suggestion to a subject that everyone else in the room has left and that all the chairs are now empty, that only the subject and the operator remain in the room. The subject is then told to open his eyes. He sees no one else present. He has a negative hallucination for the people present and a positive one in that he can see the empty chairs which are actually occupied.

An amusing incident occurred once when I was demonstrating this to a group of several physicians. The subject was the fiancee of one of those present. She was seated on a couch with her fiance on her right and one of the physicians on her left. When she was given the suggestion that her boyfriend had left the room, she opened her eyes and was unable to see him. Interested in this, he placed his hand on her knee. She then turned very indignantly to the surprised doctor on her left and scolded him for being familiar and putting *his* hand on her knee.

Sometimes *amnesia* occurs, when a person in a deep state of hypnosis awakens and has no conscious memory of what happened while he was hypnotized. This may occur spontaneously. It can be induced by suggestion, by telling the subject he will not remember when awakened. Suggestion, on the other hand, can also prevent amnesia from developing, causing the subject to remember everything.

The suggested amnesia can be only partial if that is suggested. The subject can be told he will remember everything except one specific thing. Sometimes during hypnotherapy a patient may be led to bring out something very frightening that is too overwhelming to be consciously remembered at that time. The operator will then suggest amnesia for this upon awakening, until the patient can be led to be able to tolerate the knowledge.

Certain *physical controls* are possible under hypnosis. Apparently the subconscious part of the mind controls the entire physical mechanism of the body. This is carried out through the brain and the nervous system. It seems the inner mind can influence the action of the organs and glands, of circulation, and probably of chemical changes in the body. There has been little research on these possibilities but some have been demonstrated. Sometimes suggestions can be helpful in illnesses where some malfunction of organs or glands can be affected. For instance, it has been shown that the heartbeat can either be slowed down or speeded up by hypnotic suggestion, with cardiograms taken to demonstrate this.

Control of blood circulation can often be demonstrated. Suggestion can cause one hand to blanch, with decreased flow of blood into it, while the other hand will flush from excess flow. Aaron Moss, a prominent dentist and authority/lecturer on "hypnodontics," sometimes places himself in self-hypnosis while lecturing. With his own suggestions he will show this ability, one hand blanching and the other flushing when held out in front of him.

Being flat-chested and lacking good bust development can be a psychologically upsetting matter with some young women. It is definitely possible with hypnotic suggestion to cause increase in bust development, requiring a period of about three months. A number of girl subjects have been able to develop bust measurement increases of from one to two-and-a-half inches when given proper suggestions. This may well be possible with self-hypnosis, for I know of one young woman who informed me she gained almost two inches with her own suggestions.

There could be no harm from self-suggestions for this. For the benefit of girl readers who might wish to undertake this, the suggestions I have used are given here. With the subject in hypnosis I mention that before reaching maturity she had no breast development. When she began to mature, hormonal and other changes took place and her breast developed. With some girls this process stopped too soon, before their busts had reached a satisfactory size. I suggest that this same process will now be renewed, will begin again, and will continue until the breasts have developed to the size desired. I suggest better circulation of the blood in the area, bringing increased nourishment to the tissues. I add that she will often feel increased warmth and perhaps mild tingling sensations there. It is difficult to know whether this is actually what takes place, but bust development certainly does follow.

In working with a group of girls this way, a physician friend of mine and I found that with some of the girls there were certain psychological factors working at the time of maturation which seemed to have prevented good bust development. With insight into these factors, the attempt was made to correct them. One, for instance, was a rejection of femininity by the girl, wishing she was a boy instead, partly because her parents had wanted a boy and had let her know this at an early age.

Hypnosis has been used in many other ways to cause physical changes in conditions caused by emotional and psychological factors. It is frequently used for weight reduction with obese or overweight patients, as explained in a later chapter.

The one hypnotic phenomenon only discovered in recent times is *time distortion.* This was first noted by the late Lynn Cooper, M.D., of Washington, D.C. He first wrote of it in a scientific article and then, with Dr. Milton Erickson, published an interesting book about it.

There are some conscious incidents where time seems to be distorted. People who have been saved at the last moment from drowning have reported apparently reliving long experiences of their past life. At a conscious level, time can seem to go very slowly when we are bored or are impatiently waiting for some expected event to happen. The opposite is true when we are engrossed in something interesting. Thus, time seems to be either expanded or contracted.

The subconscious mind seems to possess a very accurate time clock. Many people seem to have the ability to awaken at some early hour if that is necessary, "setting" themselves like an alarm clock is set.

In hypnosis, time can be distorted to an extreme degree. This can occur while the subject is in hypnosis or even afterwards as a post-hypnotic suggestion. Dr. Cooper would tell the hypnotized subject of his research that he would set a metronome to beat at the rate of once a minute. He would give the subject a problem to solve, either a mental or a physical task. The subject was then told to solve this within ten minutes – ten beats of the metronome. Actually the metronome was set to beat once a second instead of once a minute, so that time was distorted at a sixty times greater rate. The problem would be solved within that time.

A psychiatrist taking one of our courses for professional men practiced at home, using his ten-year-old son as a subject. With the boy in hypnosis, he told him to hallucinate, to see again a motion picture which they had seen a few days before. He then said he would awaken the boy in ten minutes. As he watched his son, the boy suddenly began to lift his right hand up to his face, repeating this very rapidly, as though waving the entire arm. The father wondered why this was done but said nothing until he awakened the boy a few moments later. Then he asked what the boy was doing, lifting his hand to his face in this rapid motion.

"Oh," said his son, "I was in the theater eating popcorn."

The father then realized what he had done. He had told the boy to see a two-hour motion picture in ten minutes, thus producing time distortion.

Time distortion is easily produced by almost any very good subject. Children are such good subjects that they can distort time very readily while under hypnosis. In demonstrating in our classes we often will use a child as a subject and will have him see a hallucinated television program which perhaps lasted an actual half hour while the operator counts to ten, which is about ten seconds.

One of the instructors with Hypnosis Symposiums is a physician who is also a concert pianist. He usually rises at five in the morning and practices for two hours at the piano. Sometimes when he cannot take the time he will use self-hypnosis, at which he is excellent. He will then distort time and will mentally practice playing for a few moments. He seems to have as good results from these few moments of mental practice as he obtains from two hours of physical practice.

Time distortion is sometimes used in hypnotherapy in connection with age regression. The patient is told while in hypnosis to regress to some important experience and relive it in just ten seconds, although the actual time involved may have been fifteen or twenty minutes, or even longer.

Sometimes an operator may be able, through hypnotic suggestion, to inhibit or prevent muscular movements. It is easier to cause this in smaller groups of muscles than in larger ones. It may be suggested that one arm is becoming heavy, so heavy that the subject will be unable to move it. After repetitions of this idea he is invited to try, but reminded that he cannot succeed in moving the arm. Visible efforts may then be seen, but the arm cannot be lifted.

A somewhat similar demonstration is for the operator to ask the subject to extend his arm and make all its muscles tight. It is then suggested that he will be unable to bend the arm, that the elbow and wrist joints are locked, and the arm cannot be bent. The operator can then try to cause the arm to bend and can even exert great pressure, but the arm will remain as rigid as a bar of iron.

In order to arouse laughter from his audience, a stage hypnotist may suggest to a hypnotized subject that he return to his seat, but that he will be unable to sit down. He can try but his knees will not bend. His waist will remain unbent no matter how he tries to sit down. The contortions the subject will then go through in trying to sit are usually quite funny and, of course, he is unsuccessful.

At least a medium depth, perhaps about twenty inches on our imaginary yardstick described later, is needed in order for a subject to produce *hallucinations*. Any of the five senses can be hallucinated by suggestion. It is harder to induce visual hallucinations than those of the other senses. A deep stage of hypnosis is required for this as a rule, and is also required for auditory hallucinations. Smell, taste, and touch may require only a medium depth. Negative and positive suggested hallucinations have already been described.

The senses may also be affected in other ways than by hallucination. Total blindness and total deafness have been produced temporarily in hypnotized subjects. There have been several experimental tests made along these lines.

It has been reported but never scientifically proven that hypnotic suggestion can cause greatly increased acuity of any of the senses. This has even been reported as developing spontaneously in some subjects. It has been claimed that a hypnotized person given proper suggestions can hear a pin dropped to the floor at a distance of several feet. It should be easy to test such claims by scientifically controlled tests, but no one has taken the trouble to carry them out.

4
The Use of Suggestion and Auto-Suggestion

Suggestion can be defined as the process of uncritically accepting an idea for belief or action. If we were not suggestible, it would be difficult to learn, and children are very suggestible because it is essential for them to learn readily.

Sometimes suggestibility is confused with gullibility, the quality of being easily fooled. It is an asset to be suggestible rather than rigid and unbelieving, whereas gullibility is a liability. It is interesting to note that we tend to accept and believe the written word, hence being more suggestible to written material than to what is heard. There is more authority and validity in something we read rather than in what is said to us.

In medical research the results of suggestion are very important. In testing the action of drugs, the placebo effect must always be considered and avoided. A placebo is an inert substance, such as a sugar pill, which would have no physical effect. With such experiments, one group of subjects is given the drug being tested, another, called a control group, is given a placebo. The subjects must not know if they are receiving the real drug or the placebo. In fact, it has been found that tests must be "double blind." Even those giving the drug and the placebo must not know which group receives the placebo or the subjects may pick up information from minimal cues unconsciously given by the experimenters, and would react as though they had received the actual drug, due to the effect of suggestion.

Suggestion continually affects our behavior. Knowing something about it and the ways to make it most effective can be of definite value in helping you increase your ability to study well. The subconscious part of the mind can be influenced with suggestion so your learning ability is increased. A more suggestible individual makes the best hypnotic subject, which is one of the main reasons why children are such good subjects. Four out of five children between the ages of five and thirteen will reach a deep trance.

There have been tests devised to help learn the degree of a subject's suggestibility. In general, they are also tests of hypnotizability, for suggestibility and hypnotizability go hand in hand. Some operators make preliminary use of one or two tests before an induction, though most do not bother with them. One reason is that many tests are challenges, and a person may react to a challenge by carrying out what the operator has suggested cannot be done.

Suggestions made by someone else are called

hetero-suggestions. These are usually more effective than auto-suggestion. However, this does not mean that suggestions you give yourself are not effective; they usually are. We are much more suggestible when in hypnosis, and this applies to either hetero or self-suggestion. Suggestibility increases with greater depths of hypnosis. The subconscious part of the mind tends to accept suggestions better when you are deeply hypnotized.

Suggestions may be given with positive wording, or the wording may be negative. The former has much greater effect. It is better to say "you will" rather than "you won't." In wording suggestions which are to be given, avoid words such as *won't, don't, can't,* and similar ones which are all negative. Sometimes negative wording can't be avoided, but usually you can think of wording which will be positive. Avoid using the word *try* in giving suggestions. Telling a person to try to do something implies doubt and failure. The subject is not to try, he is to do it, whatever is involved in the suggestion.

The wording and manner in which a suggestion is given can be in a commanding or permissive way. Essentially this is by using the phrase "you will" for a command and "you can" as permissive. This may affect the acceptance of the idea. A person who is very dependent might accept a command more readily than he would a permissive suggestion. On the other hand, many people do not like to be ordered to do something and, with resentment, will rebel and pay no attention to such a suggestion. This situation is of more importance when dealing with someone who is not in hypnosis. Under hypnosis a subject would be more apt to accept a command, due to the factor of rapport — the desire to please and cooperate with the hypnotist.

Suggestions may be direct or indirect. A direct one is more likely to be weighed and possibly not accepted. Indirect suggestion is more subtle and may escape both conscious and subconscious censorship, hence then being accepted and carried out.

Perhaps the most important rule involved in making suggestions effective is that of repetition. The idea to be impressed on the subconscious should be repeated a number of times. Advertising is based on suggestion and all advertisers are well aware of the importance of repetition, which is cumulative in force. Television commercials are one of the most obvious examples of this. The advantages of the advertised article are pounded home to the TV viewer again and again. It pays the advertiser. Sometimes, in my own personal opinion, advertising agencies overlook the fact that too much repetition can bring a kick-back, in that the viewer begins to resent the oft-repeated commercial and will make a point not to buy an article where repetition has become almost nauseating.

The wording of any suggestion should always be clear and literal because the subconscious will certainly take the literal meaning, which may not be what you meant to impart.

There are several techniques which help make suggestions more likely to be accepted. If some emotion can be aroused in connection with a suggestion, it adds emphasis, though sometimes it is not feasible to bring in any emotion. Visual imagery can sometimes be used to stir up some emotion.

Visual imagery of any result will make any suggestion more effective, remembering the need for repetition. For instance, in treating obesity, a therapist usually tells his patient to visualize herself standing in front of a mirror, seeing herself in the glass as slender. In helping a girl develop her bust, she is told to visualize her breasts as she wants them to be.

In wording any suggestion, put the time for it to be carried out in the future, rather than in the present tense. This can be the very immediate future — "very soon," — "in a few minutes." This allows time for the idea to be absorbed.

It is best not to burden the subconscious with several suggestions in any one session. Two or no more than three is best.

The subject's inner mind may or may not accept the ideas presented. Using the ideomotor questioning technique which will be dealt with later, it is possible to ask if the inner mind will carry out what has been suggested. If an affirmative answer is given, in all probability success will result unless something unforeseen interferes. The subconscious tends to carry out such a commitment.

During the 1920's a pharmacist in Nancy, France named Emil Coué became interested and made an intensive study of suggestion. He put his ideas into practice and established a suggestion "clinic." Results were so excellent that people came to him from all over Europe. He taught his patients how to use autosuggestion, and the main phrase he advocated using became world famous— "Every day in every way I'm getting better and better."

Coué had worked this out carefully. It states only the end result desired, puts it into immediate effect, although not stating the moment, and leaves the means of accomplishment of the desired end up to the subconscious mind. The patient was told to repeat this phrase to himself every morning, on going to bed at night, and several times during the day. Many persons benefited.

Coué made a lecture tour of the United States, or rather he began one and quickly gave it up. Skeptical newspaper men ridiculed him, poked fun at his methods, and changed his phrase to "Hell's bells, I'm well." Coué found little acceptance here as a result, but nevertheless his ideas are sound. He pointed out many of the matters discussed here and the ways of making suggestion most effective.

He also formulated several laws about suggestion. One is the *Law of Reversed Effect.* Coué says that whenever one is in doubt about something, the harder he tries to accomplish it, the less he is able. An example would be to lay a ten-foot board one foot wide on the floor. If told to walk it, a person would do it hardly even glancing at the board. Place the board between two chairs about three feet from the floor and there will still be no difficulty, though more care is taken. If the same board is placed between the windows of two buildings ten stories high, the person probably could not even start to walk it, and if he did his doubts and the law working would probably cause him to fall.

Another law stated by Coué was the *Law of Concentrated Attention.* When spontaneous attention is concentrated on an idea, the subconscious mind tends to carry it out. Coué also said that when imagination (the subconscious) and the will (the conscious mind) are in conflict, imagination invariably wins.

An American follower of Coué, Frederick Pierce, added another law, the *Law of Dominant Effect,* which states that an idea always tends toward realization. The mind always pays attention to the strongest feeling or emotion which is present. If a person experiences a feeling of happiness and pleasure but danger arises, danger is the stronger emotion and the pleasurable feeling is instantly snuffed out.

The hypnotizability of people varies greatly. Only a very few persons seem unhypnotizable for various reasons. This depends partly on the skill of the hypnotist. A beginner might find one in ten unsusceptible, where an experienced operator would probably meet with 95 percent success. Another important factor here is motivation. A dentist will have the best success with his patients due to their desire to escape from the pain and discomforts of dental treatment.

As a general statement, it can be said that 5 percent are not hypnotizable; about 30 percent will enter a light trance; approximately 50 percent will reach a medium depth; and 15 percent will enter the deep stage. These figures would apply to an average population. If hypnotizability were to be graphed by age, the graph line would begin at about three years of age, would ascend to a peak at six, and begin a very gradual descent at about ten. Elderly people are usually the hardest to hypnotize, but this varies greatly with the individual.

Some time ago, an eighty-year-old woman made an appointment to see me. When she arrived at my office she was accompanied by another woman of about the same age. My patient asked that her friend be present, or she did not want to be hypnotized. Of course I agreed. When I had finished an induction talk and my patient had reached quite a deep state, I happened to look at her friend. She too had gone into a deep hypnotic state and was hardly being a good chaperone!

Tests have shown that there is no difference in hypnotizability between the sexes, although my observation is that women may be more willing to be hypnotized, perhaps more curious, and less afraid. There also seems to be no difference among races. Those accustomed to being led are more likely to be good subjects than are leaders. An army private will probably be a better subject than an officer, but again individuals vary widely. All these are only broad statements. It used to be thought that the insane could not be hypnotized. Since many psychiatrists now use hypnosis, it has been learned that this is not so and that many psychotics *can* enter hypnosis. The exception here is the paranoia case, who seldom can be hypnotized because of his suspicions.

It is possible to test suggestibility and also hypnotizability, as several tests are available. One is termed the *sway test*. The subject is asked to stand with his eyes closed. The operator stands beside him or just behind him. Suggestions are given with wording similar to the following:

"Now let your knees be stiff, your whole body rigid and erect. With your eyes closed look up toward the ceiling, but without tilting your head back. You cannot fall because I am right here to catch you but you will soon find yourself falling backward. You will have a feeling of wanting to fall backwards. Do not resist. You are swaying now, swaying slightly back and then forward, now swaying backwards more and more. You are falling back, back, falling backwards, falling, falling!"

The operator must be prepared to catch the subject, no matter which direction he falls. Strangely, about one in twenty will fall forward instead of backward. Perhaps he is willing to fall but unconsciously wants to do so in his own way. Most people will respond to these suggestions and fall backwards. A good percentage will even go into hypnosis in doing so. Most, but not all, will fall backwards a considerable distance if allowed to by the operator, and will not step back with one foot as they fall, something almost impossible to do voluntarily.

Two other tests are commonly used — one an eye closure test and the other a handclasp test. These are somewhat similar and are induced with much the same wording. The subject is asked to close his eyes and squeeze the lids tightly together. He is then asked to look upwards but not to tilt his head back. The working of the suggestions given could be as follows:

"I am going to count to three and you will be unable to open your eyes. Wait until I tell you when to try and then try hard, but the harder you try the tighter your eyelids will stick together. One, your eyelids are sticking together tightly. Squeeze them tightly together. They are gluing fast together. Two, your eyelids are welded together now, welded tightly together. Three, the lids are locked tightly together. You couldn't possibly open them. Now try, but you cannot get them apart. They are tight, tight, tight. Now stop trying. You could open your eyes, but let them stay closed."

The handclasp test is rather similar. The subject is told to lace his fingers together and press the palms together. The wording is the same as above, but hands are substituted for eyes.

These tests can be made either with a person awake or in hypnosis, and stage hypnotists often use them in order to select good subjects for their performance. Of course, they are more successful when the person is in hypnosis.

Tests of this nature are challenges. Some people will respond to a challenge by doing whatever they are told they cannot do, and this may be true even under hypnosis. To avoid a challenge it is possible to tell the subject that you want him to see how he can respond to his own suggestions, that you will tell him what to say as suggestions to himself. Then the wording as above is used but instead of using the word "you," "I" is substituted and the subject gives himself the suggestions. There is no challenge and the results are usually much better.

How is the depth of hypnosis reached by a subject determined? An experienced hypnotist can usually sense this in some way, mainly through what he observes in the subject's behavior and through his experience with hypnosis. The only scientific way to determine depth is to make a series of tests to determine what hypnotic phenomena the subject will produce.

Certain phenomena are considered obtainable in each stage of depth. Actually this will vary a good deal with the individual subject. Sometimes something attributed to only a light state cannot be induced even if the subject is in a deep trance. Conversely, one in a light state might produce some deep trance phenomenon.

Here are some of the factors usually relegated to a light state — catalepsy of the eyes, partial limb catalepsy, slower breathing and slower pulse, disinclination to move or speak, rapport with the operator, and feeling of heaviness or perhaps the opposite — a floating feeling, response to simple post-hypnotic suggestions, and partial age regressions.

In a medium state, there is more recognition of being hypnotized, muscular inhibitions, partial amnesia, glove anesthesia, some illusions, and complete body catalepsy.

The deep trance is marked by the ability to open the eyes without awakening (sometimes possible in a medium state); a fixed stare with eyes open; complete amnesia; post-hypnotic amnesia; post-hypnotic anesthesia; bizarre post-hypnotic suggestions heeded; and control of organic body functions such as circulation, hypermnesia, complete age regression, visual or auditory hallucinations, or time distortion.

In most scientific research, the depth of hypnosis in subjects is usually measured by the Stanford Hypnotic Susceptibility Scales and Stanford Profile Scales of Hypnotic Susceptibility. These are tests involving loss of voluntary control (as in challenges), motor suggestions such as the sway test, and phenomena such as hallucinations, amnesia, and post-hypnotic responses. Some other depth scales not in present use are the Davis and Husband scale and the LeCron-Bordeaux scale.

Since these methods of depth measurement require much time and cannot be used as a quick, accurate way of measuring depth, they are not too satisfactory. With this in mind I tried to devise a quick, accurate method. Realizing the many abilities of the inner mind, it seemed that this part of the mind might itself be able to determine depth if given a yardstick with which to measure. In other words, perhaps the patient himself could tell how deep he was through the use of the questioning technique to be explained shortly.

We can say that a light stage of hypnosis is the first foot, one to twelve inches, on an imaginary yardstick. A medium state is the second foot. twelve to twenty-four inches, and twenty-four to thirty-six inches represents the deep state. With this imaginary yardstick the subconscious can measure and then tell us the depth the subject has reached.

In hypnosis a certain depth is not continually maintained. There is a fluctuation. At one moment a person may be deeper than at another moment. The questions asked of the subconscious should go something as follows: first, the yardstick is explained to the subject while he is in hypnosis. Then he is asked, "Have you been as deep or deeper in this session than twenty inches on our yardstick?" If the answer is affirmative, the next question would correspond to twenty-five inches. If the reply is negative, it would correspond to fifteen inches. A bracket of five inches is quite sufficient.

It should be said that this method of measurement has been thoroughly checked for accuracy by others as well as myself. It only takes a very short time to obtain the needed information of depth. The method of measurement has been taught to several thousand who have taken the Hypnosis Symposium courses and today is in wide usage.

Still another way of obtaining the information of depth, also using the yardstick method, is to ask the hypnotized subject to visualize immediately in front of him an imaginary yardstick set on end with the one-inch mark at the top. Pointing at the top, he is to see a white arrow indicator. As he watches, this indicator is to slide down the yardstick and stop at the greatest depth he has reached. He can then read the inch mark and report it.

5
Your
Subconscious Mind

A number of different names have been given to the inner part of the mind — the "unconscious," "subconscious," "subliminal," "subjective," and various other terms. The most commonly accepted term in psychotherapy is "unconscious." Preferably to many is "subconscious," which has only one meaning. Unconscious has two, meaning the inner mind or a period of being "out" — unconsciousness.

Even the ancient Greeks knew there is an inner part of the mind, but Freud's work was the first that led to a degree of understanding about it. We still know little of that area. Many people do not realize that it is capable of thinking and reasoning, although it does this in a different manner than the conscious mind. This is readily shown by means of the ideomotor question-answering technique which is described later.

That part of the mind is the storehouse of memory. Age regression proves how even the most minor detail is registered in memory. It might be compared to the making of a tape recording combined with a motion picture or video-tape with sight and sound registered, plus the other three senses. All can be replayed through age regression.

There have been different theories formulated as to the actual makeup of the inner mind. Most commonly accepted is the Freudian theory, although it fails to cover everything about that part of the mind. Freud believed the total unconscious to be composed of what he termed the *id* or our basic instincts; the pre-conscious, which is just below conscious awareness; and the super-ego, which is essentially the conscience. The part of the mind which is our awareness he called the "ego."

The late psychiatrist Anita Muhl is known as the greatest authority on automatic writing. Briefly, it consists of the subconscious controlling the subject's hand and writing while the subject is unaware of what is being written. With this, Dr. Muhl found she could contact seven different layers or levels of the inner mind, which ranged from what could be described as "the devil," "the Old Nick," or some similar term, and which seemed much like Freud's id, to the super-ego, though she found this to correspond more to Carl Jung's idea of a super-consciousness. One of the other levels seemed to deal with our self-protection, and still another was the memory level. Another had to do with control of bodily processes.

Another theory about the subconscious compares it to a mechanical computer, this idea being first advanced by Norbert Weiner and described by Maxwell Maltz in his book *Psycho-cybernetics* (Prentice-Hall, Englewood Cliffs, N.J.).

This theory holds that the subconscious is completely mechanistic, working through the brain. Because of its tremendous abilities, comparing the subconscious to the most elaborate computer would be like comparing a huge printing press to a rubber-stamp. This theory seems to deny the ability of the subconscious to reason.

This inner part of the mind often seems to operate in a very illogical way. It is concerned only with end results in its motivations and consequent behavior, entirely disregarding possible side effects which may be very detrimental. At times it seems to be very immature and childish. It tends to be without humor, although in automatic writing it often puns in an amusing way.

The subconscious takes everything literally — whatever it hears. This can cause complications and sometimes results in our behavior becoming detrimental to us. Here we are in semantics. In some of our speech, we say something having an entirely different literal meaning to what we intended to say. For example, if angry we may say, "That makes me mad." We only mean that we are angry but literally we have said we are insane.

This literalness of the subconscious is evident with a hypnotized person, the subconscious then being nearer the surface so we are dealing with it more directly. If a person in hypnosis is asked the question, "Would you tell me where you were born?" he will answer by nodding his head or saying "yes." Literally that is the correct answer. If awake, he would name the place where he was born, interpreting the question. Realization of this literalness is important in wording suggestions. It is sometimes the source of imprints which are described later.

A very detrimental example of such an imprint is

often located during hypnotherapy when therapy seems to fail and there is no result in the attempt to rid a patient of some illness or condition. There are several phrases which will act to block progress if they become imprinted in the subconscious. Some of these are "Nothing will do any good" and "You'll never get over this;" a much worse one is "You'll have to learn to live with this." Doctors may fail to help a patient when using orthodox medical treatment and may make such a remark, not realizing its possible result.

This last phrase may appear quite harmless and would be unless it becomes an imprint. If it is said when the patient is frightened, despairing, or under some other emotion, he may be in hypnosis and certainly is very suggestible. If the subconscious accepts this idea, the condition is locked up so it can't be removed. What is the literal meaning of "You'll have to learn to live with this"? Actually it means that if the condition or symptom is ended, then the patient will die! If you do not learn to live with it, you'll be dead. Not wishing to die, the subconscious holds on to the condition desperately.

The inner mind seems to continue to view any experience with the viewpoint held at the time of its occurrence. If something of importance occurred at five years old, it keeps on regarding this as would a five-year-old. Consciously our views change as we mature and gain experience. What might seem very frightening to a child might even be amusing as an adult.

If a young child is shut in a dark closet as a punishment for some misdeed and becomes very frightened, he may develop a fear of the dark, or a fear of enclosed places (claustrophobia) which persists throughout his life. Consciously, he would wonder why he becomes panicky in such a situation, which to an adult seems silly. The childhood view is subconsciously still in effect.

One important duty of the subconscious is to protect us. If you touch something hot so that you are burned, you do not stop to think that you must take your hand from the hot object. That would take too long and damage would be greater. The subconscious instantly reacts to the pain of the burn and the muscles snatch the hand away instantly.

This part of the mind is always on duty, while we are asleep, even if unconscious as from general anesthesia in surgery, or when knocked out. Physicians are only beginning to learn that this is true, since it has been pointed out to them by colleagues who know hypnosis. A person can be age-regressed to an operation and will be able to relate whatever happened while he was unconscious, if it had any importance to him. The conscious part of the mind is "out" but the inner mind is continuously functioning.

A good example of the alertness of the inner mind during sleep is seen with the mother of an infant. Although deeply asleep, she hears and will awaken at once if the baby even whimpers. The subconscious awakens her to see if anything dangerous is happening to the child.

Another way the subconscious functions is at times to punish us (masochism) when guilt feelings are developed due to some transgression. Strangely, and showing something of its lack of logic, one part of the subconscious may lead us to "sin" or do something wrong which we regret. Then another part, the conscience, goes to work and slaps us down for having done it!

Still another function of that part of the mind is to regulate the physical mechanism of the body, working through the brain and the nervous system. Research has shown this true as to some functioning of glands and organs.

It is important to know something about this inner part of the mind and the way it operates. Then it can be more easily affected.

It should not be thought from these explanations and from what you learn later with ideomotor replies to questions, that it is as though there was another person inside you. That is not the proper concept. The total person is a unit with the mind in two parts, each influencing the other. You are a complete individual. A comparison has been made that the mind is like an iceberg floating in the sea. The conscious part is that above the water. The subconscious is below the water and is about four-fifths of the total.

6
Obtaining Information
from
Your Subconscious Mind

Psychotherapists who work with hypnosis quickly learn to have great respect for the abilities of the inner mind. Its knowledge stored in memory is prodigious. Every detail observed is registered in the memory and much can be brought to consciousness through hypnosis that is not otherwise available.

Sometime ago I had as a patient a twenty-five- year old man. Under hypnosis he was age-regressed to the age of eight months to bring out a trauma at that age which was still affecting him. He told of being in a crib in his bedroom and described the room in great detail – the number and arrangement of the windows, the pictures on the wall, the color and design of the carpet. He remembered all this on awakening and discussed it with his mother. She was amazed and informed me that he had described the room perfectly though they had sold this house, including the furniture when he was a year old. Yet all this had registered in his memory.

In regressions of this type subjects regressed to a very early age will report what they heard said by people present. Sometimes a remark has acted as an imprint, with persistent effects. Since at early ages a child does not know language, is such a report only fantasy? Many psychotherapists believe there has been a recording made in memory much like a tape recording. What might be said is registered only as sounds, the meaning not known at the time. When language is learned the subconscious then interprets the sounds and they have meaning. This would seem to be the only possible explanation, if these apparent memories are not fantasy.

One of the reasons why hypnosis is so valuable in psychotherapy is because so many forgotton memories can easily be brought out with it, memories of experiences which cause trouble to the person. We tend to repress anything which has been very unpleasant or frightening, pushing them out of the conscious mind. We often suppress guilt feelings, not wanting to think about them. Subconsciously, such feelings and memories may fester and the inner mind may call for self-punishment. Then we wonder why we have hurt ourselves "accidentally," or have developed some painful illness such as arthritis or headaches.

Factories with large numbers of employees have found that 80 percent of all accidents happen to only 20 percent of the employees, an indication of how prevalent unconsciously motivated "accidents" may be. Of course, some are strictly accidental.

As has been stated, the subconscious part of the mind thinks and reasons. Consciously, we reason both inductively and deductively. The inner mind seems only to reason deductively.

It is valuable to be able more readily to influence the subconscious through hypnosis. Even more important is to be able to tap the knowledge in that part of our mental makeup, to learn from it things not consciously known. This can be done while a person is awake or while in hypnosis.

By wording questions so they can be answered "yes" or "no," it is possible to set up a code of communication with the subconscious, which can answer them by signals. If you nod your head in answer to a question, you are replying with a signal. Subconsciously controlled movements with an idea involved are called *ideomotor movements*. There are two ways of obtaining signal answers to questions.

One way is to use some light object such as a finger ring, earring, iron washer, or anything light. Tie a thread about ten inches long to it. Holding the thread between the thumb and forefinger, let the weight dangle freely. It then forms a pendulum. Your arm can be rested on the arm of a chair or on a table, or on your knee while you lean slightly forward. The subconscious can then control your fingers to move the pendulum without you moving it voluntarily. You should try to hold it motionless. It will operate better if you watch the object. Movement of your fingers in causing the object to swing will be so slight as to be imperceptible.

The pendulum can swing in four basic directions. It can move in a clockwise circle, a counterclockwise circle, straight across in front of you, or back and forth away from you.

Each of the four movements can have a meaning. One can mean *yes*, another *no*, the third can signify *I don't know*, and the remaining can mean *I don't want to answer the question*. Sometimes the latter is important. Questions will usually receive a reply unless they are about something unpleasant or frightening which the inner mind doesn't want disturbed.

As you hold the pendulum so it dangles freely, ask

your subconscious mind to select one of the movements which is to mean the affirmative. Then think the word "yes" several times to yourself. Try to hold the pendulum still, but almost invariably you will find it will begin to swing. The movement may be slight but definite, or it may move in a good-sized arc. Do not think how you want it to move, but let your subconscious make its own selection. Sometimes it takes a few moments to "warm up the motor" before the pendulum begins to swing. Often it will start to move immediately.

When this answer has been established, then ask for a motion which will mean "no." With this signal set up, then ask for "I don't know." The remaining motion will then mean "not wanting to answer," but this should be stated to your inner mind. You do not need to ask your questions verbally, just think them.

In my experience and that of many other psychotherapists and physicians who have learned how to use this ideomotor technique, only with perhaps three or four people out of one hundred will the pendulum fail to move. In this case it invariably means subconscious resistance for some reason. There may be something it fears will be brought out, or there may be some other reason for resistance. Trying again at another time may bring the movements. With a very few people, questions may be answered if someone other than yourself asks them, when you are unable to get responses yourself.

While a person is in hypnosis with his eyes closed it is easier to resort to another technique. It also may be used in the waking state. This is by finger movements; be sure you do not move them voluntarily. The subconscious can be asked to select any four of the ten fingers, using the same four replies to questioning. It is probably a bit easier to watch and keep track of the movements if four fingers of one hand are used. You could specify the forefinger for affirmative, middle finger for negative, little finger for not knowing, and the thumb for not wanting to answer.

With some people it may be possible to secure replies with the pendulum, but for some reason the fingers will not move, or maybe vice versa. The fingers will answer questions but the pendulum only hangs motionless. With at least nineteen out of twenty persons both methods work.

With the finger technique, when a finger is about to lift, the subject usually feels a tingling sensation in the muscles. When the control is involuntary the finger invariably trembles or wiggles and lifts very slowly, perhaps moving only slightly. Others may find the movement slow but the finger will lift higher into a pointing position. In using this method the hands or hand should rest flat on the arm of your chair, in your lap, or on your legs. Everyone finds these ideomotor movements of the pendulum or fingers quite fascinating.

In using this technique as a means of getting information from the inner mind, you may find the pendulum swinging in a diagonal direction or an undesignated finger lifting. This again, shows that the subconscious is reasoning. It indicates that that part of the mind is trying to answer but cannot do so with the four basic motions. This may signify *perhaps* or *maybe,* or it may be that your question is not clear or is worded so it is not understood. You can find the meaning by asking questions to what it does signify.

With ideomotor responses to questions, how much can the replies be trusted? Are they to be depended on as correct? Unless the inner mind has some definite reason for misleading you — which is most unlikely — the answers given will be correct. That part of the mind seems to prefer to signal that it doesn't want to answer a question rather than to give false information. It is only sensible, however, to feel there is always a bare possibility of wishful thinking causing the answer to be misleading, and to use common sense in accepting all answers as valid.

Some have asked questions regarding the future, trying to have the subconscious prognosticate. Asking your subconscious to pick the winner of a horse race may be expensive! Replies will only be accurate if the knowledge is in the inner mind, though it might try to please you by answering such a question. In parapsychology there are some indications that this part of the mind might have some knowledge of the future, but it has never been proved scientifically. To depend in any way on it having such knowledge would be foolish.

It is possible to use this technique to locate lost articles, provided always that your subconscious knows what happened to such an article. It may also be used sometimes to decide for you when there are two or more options to some action — when you are not sure what course you should take. As its data in memory is much more than you can remember consciously, it may be able to give you the answer to the best course to follow.

In rare instances, people have become so fascinated with this way of obtaining information from the inner mind that they have gone somewhat overboard and used it improperly. One woman asked her subconscious if her husband had been unfaithful to her. Of course that part of her mind had no means of knowing this. Probably it tried to oblige her by giving the answer, which was affirmative. She would not have asked such a question if she had not anticipated an affirmative reply. Her husband told me she had always been very jealous, and denied ever having "stepped out." This almost broke up their marriage. Questioning should never be considered to bring valid answers unless the questions are about something definitely known to the inner part of the mind. While an answer to some other type of question might be received, it would be foolish to trust it or assume it is true.

You may be surprised at times when asking questions, to find your subconscious signalling "no" to some question you are certain has an affirmative answer, and vice versa. In all probability the subconscious reply is the correct one.

There is really nothing magical or mysterious in these ideomotor movements. The subconscious continually controls muscular movements. Your breathing is a good example. When you walk, you do not consciously think of all the coordination of the various muscles involved in walking. You had to learn this as a child, at first giving it conscious effort, and falling many times. Then as you learned, your subconscious took control. It is very easy for it to manipulate your fingers, either to lift them or to cause the pendulum to swing.

It is important to know how to ask questions properly and just what to ask. Of course, this depends on your particular aims. Some examples will be given, and from them you can learn to select proper wording for whatever you may wish to ask. In experimenting, you might try asking questions aloud, and also merely thinking them. With most everyone it seems to make no difference but, with a few, verbal questioning seems more effective. Some cannot seem

to get answers to their own questions, but will if someone
else does the asking.

Taken from a tape recording, here is the way
questioning was conducted in one of my cases. This will vary
considerably in each case, but in asking your own questions
you would use the first person in the wording.

The patient was a twenty-year-old college student
who was having great difficulty in his studies. His earlier
grades had not been good enough to be admitted to a large
university, so he was attending a small college.

Q. Is there anything working in your subconscious mind
    which is acting in any way to affect your ability to learn
    easily?
A. Yes [these were pendulum replies].
Q. Is it in regard to studying?
A. Yes.
Q. Does it prevent you from getting better grades?
A. Yes.
Q. There could be several things involved. Does it have to do
    with your memory? Does it affect your ability to
    remember?
A. No.
Q. Does it affect your ability to concentrate well?
A. Yes.
Q. Is this why your mind tends to wander when you try to
    study?
A. Yes.
Q. Is the reason for this that you are punishing yourself for
    some reason in failing to get good grades?
A. No.
Q. Do you feel unworthy or inferior so that you can't use all
    of your mental abilities?
A. No.

Q. Is it one or more imprints which are affecting you? [imprints had been explained to him].

A. Yes.

Q. Are there more than one of these imprints?

A. Yes.

Q. More than two?

A. Yes.

Q. More than three?

A. No.

Q. Let's consider the first one in point of the time when it originated. Was this something you heard said?

A. Yes.

Q. Was it said to you? It might have been something you heard said to someone else?

A. Yes.

Q. Was it said by a male?

A. No.

Q. Then it must have been a female. It that correct?

A. Yes.

Q. Was it a teacher?

A. No.

Q. Was it a relative?

A. Yes.

Q. Was it your mother?

A. Yes.

Q. Now as to the time when this imprint originated, was it before you were fifteen years old?

A. Yes.

Q. Before ten?

A. No.

Q. Was it between ten and fifteen then?

A. Yes.

Q. Was it between ten and twelve years old?

A. No.

Q. Between twelve and fifteen?

A. Yes.

Q. Was it when you were twelve?

A. Yes.

Q. Where did this take place? Was it at your home?

A. No.

Q. At school?

A. No.

Q. At a friend's house?

A. No.

Q. At a relative's?

A. Yes.

Q. A thought will now pop into your mind as to where this took place [this was an attempt to shortcut].

A. Oh, I think it was at my aunt's.

Q. Is that correct? Was it at your aunt's?

A. Yes.

Q. We learned that your mother said this. Was she present with you at your aunt's?

A. Yes.

Q. Did it happen indoors rather than outdoors?

A. Yes.

Q. Was anyone else present?

A. Yes.

Q. Who was it? The name will pop into your mind! The first name you think of [again shortcutting].

A. Bill. That's my cousin.

Q. Was it Bill?

A. Yes.

Q. Was your mother scolding you?

A. Yes.

Q.   Did she punish you for something?

A.   Yes.

Q.   Physical punishment?

A.   No.

Q.   Did she forbid you to do something as punishment?

A.   Yes.

Q.   We need to know what was said. Was it about school or study?

A.   Yes.

Q.   Is it all right for you to remember what this was that is acting as an imprint and making it hard to study?

A.   Yes.

With age regression it was then thought out what had occurred. He had been told to do school homework but instead had gone next door to his aunt's and was playing with his cousin. His mother was angry at his disobedience. She had told him in reproaching him that he never would do any good at school. Another remark was that he never could keep his mind on what he studied. The third imprint was that he just didn't like to study, and didn't pay attention to what he was doing. Although these fixed ideas were not carried out completely, they did have the effect of hindering his abilities.

It was then impressed on his inner mind that this had happened to a boy and now he was grown and studying entirely different subjects. It was stressed that his mother was merely scolding him and had had no intention of causing such an effect for him as to prevent him from studying well. To learn if the imprints had been removed he was then asked:

Q.   Now that you understand how these imprints have hindered you, and how they have operated, can you be free of their effects?

A.   Yes.

Q.   Can you now study and learn to the best of your mental
        ability?

A.   Yes.

Another case was that of a young man twenty-one years old who came to me for help. He told me he had finished the seventh grade but had never learned to read or write. All he could do was sign his name in a crude way. I asked him how he could possibly have gone through seven grades of public school and never have learned to read and write. "Oh," he said, "I was so stupid and also so rebellious and quarrelsome that every teacher I had was so anxious to get rid of me that they passed me on to the next grade." This was in a midwestern city, which hardly speaks well for the educational system there.

Dave, as we'll call him, could only secure menial jobs and was washing dishes in a restaurant. I saw him only once when I helped him uncover the imprints that had blocked him. They had been set up by statements of an aunt who had raised him. About a year later I met him on the street, where he told me he had a girl friend who was teaching him to read and write, and was getting along very well in learning. The questions asked in bringing out his imprints were similar to the example given above.

An employee of the California motor vehicle department has told me that in giving tests for driver's licenses that it is not uncommon for an applicant to be unable to take the written part of the examination because he cannot read. Some have even graduated from high school. The law compels young people to go to school until a certain age, but evidently these non-readers have been passed on to higher grades as too stupid or too blocked to learn. The teacher wants to be rid of them, as was the case with Dave.

An interesting application of the ideomotor response to the questions technique occurred to me sometime ago and I interested several physicians in an experiment. Would the inner mind of a pregnant woman know the sex of the unborn child? This question was asked of several women and the answer was always affirmative. Four hundred and two girls and women were then asked to predict the sex of the child before they were delivered. About 90 percent of them, three hundred and sixty, predicted it correctly.

Although this experiment was not carried out scientifically, we continued it in a scientific way. The physicians asking the question about the children's sexes mailed me a postcard with the name of each woman and what sex was predicted. After the baby was delivered, they sent another card with the result. In this test the results were not nearly as good. Only two out of three had predicted correctly. This still is significant because if the answers to the questions were merely by chance, only about 50 percent would be correct. Wishful thinking could possibly enter where the girl would predict the sex she wanted — and then be wrong.

Many people complain of having a poor memory. Sometimes this is only in a general way; sometimes it is more specific, such as an inability to remember names. Probably varying degrees of intelligence enter into the ability to remember, but I wonder if imprints and repeated suggestions do not affect a great many people in memory.

In explanation of this, though proof is lacking, I suspect that we are all born with a very good memory and that it is gradually blunted as we grow up and mature. How many times do you suppose you have heard the phrases, "I don't remember," "I forget," "It slips my mind," and other words with the same meanings? It seems possible that continued repetition of these ideas could dull memory.

When it can be demonstrated so readily with hypnosis and age regression that everything that happens to us is recorded in memory in greatest detail, we should be able *consciously* to draw on these memories much better than most of us can do.

It seems to me that memory could very likely be improved for most of us if we applied Coué's method. It would be interesting to know what results would follow if you said to yourself several times a day, for a period of a month or so, the phrase "Every day my memory will improve and get better and better." It would be worthwhile to try.

As a final note on the questioning technique, It is well to write out your questions, wording them carefully, and then write down the answers which are given.

7
Induction Methods

There are many ways of inducing hypnosis, many different procedures and tactics used by different operators. Most professional people who use hypnosis usually find some method which works well for them and then use it frequently. However, the skilled operator knows many other methods and will try to fit the one he uses to the particular subject with whom he is working.

Some induction methods are authoritarian and positive, while others are entirely permissive. Obviously, it would be a mistake and invite failure to use a commanding approach with a belligerent, positive type of person. Stage hypnotists are excellent to inductions, though they may know little of the psychological aspects of hypnosis. They must use rapid induction techniques or their audience would be bored. Invariably they depend on their prestige and use a quick authoritarian type of induction. Usually a stage technique involves startling, or frightening, the volunteer subject so that he slips immediately into hypnosis.

To those in the audience the stage hypnotist is a master at induction, and indeed he is good at it. He seems able to induce a deep state in all his subjects. Actually, a part of his stock in trade is, through experience, to be able to pick people as subjects who will be excellent ones. He will call for volunteers and a number of people hurry to the stage. Looking them over quickly, he sends several back to their seats on the basis that he cannot handle so many. Of course, he is keeping those whom he thinks will be good subjects. A test is quickly made and two or three others are asked to return to their seats. Those remaining on the stage are sure to be fine subjects, and the stage operator then goes ahead with his program, often causing his subjects to do ridiculous things. Why will subjects on the stage make fools of themselves in this way? Some do so in the mistaken belief that they are in the power of the hypnotist and must do whatever they are told to do. However, if a suggestion is too obnoxious it will not be carried out, but the stage hypnotist always avoids that. Many who go up on the stage are exhibitionists who are enjoying themselves thoroughly and will then do whatever is asked of them.

Hypnosis is not something to be used for amusement and entertainment. Anyone going to the stage to be a subject is taking a chance, for few stage hypnotists really know the subject or have any knowledge of the psychological factors involved. Very few states prohibit stage exhibits, but all should do so. Medical or psychological associations often try to introduce such legislation but it usually is killed by the politicians. As a matter of fact, the United States is one of the very few countries permitting stage hypnosis. I believe Canada and Australia also permit it.

Authoritarian techniques are usually rapid in effect;

the permissive ones are slower. Formerly, most professionals preferred much slower methods than are now employed. Today it is quite possible to induce hypnosis quickly and yet be permissive and positive, but not commanding.

The majority of induction techniques vary somewhat but essentially involve eye fixation of some kind. The operator can utilize eye fixation in many ways. He can have the subject look into his eyes. He can have the subject's eyes fixed on something – a picture on the wall, a flower in a vase, the flickering flame of a candle, some bright object; almost anything will serve. The induction talk will then stress the heaviness which will come over the eye muscles and lids. After a time the subject is asked to let his eyes close. This is actually not essential but tends to shut out distractions and is usually suggested by the operator.

Further suggestions are to obtain more and more relaxation. With permissiveness the subject is always told he *can* do something, not that he *will* do it. All is on a basis of cooperation. Of course, before an induction talk is made, a subject is usually told something about hypnosis and disabused of the usual misconceptions about it.

With eye fixation methods, the subject may be told to let his eyes follow the movement of some object held in front of him. Another variation is to have him close his eyes while the operator counts, closing them on even numbers and opening again on odd numbers.

In most induction talks the operator stresses the heaviness developing in the eyelids, and the general relaxation of the body which is taking place. Some operators use the word *sleep* and talk of drowsiness, although the subject does not really go to sleep. Instead, the operator will make some distinction of hypnotic sleep.

It is quite possible to use indirect techniques which will cause the subject to become hypnotized and probably be quite unaware that he is. This can be accomplished by avoiding any mention of hypnosis, by saying that the operator would like to show the subject how to relax completely. In the induction talk relaxation is then stressed, by telling the subject to relax every muscle, either beginning at the feet and working up to the head, or reversing this and starting at the head and going on down to the feet.

Gadgets of one kind or another are sometimes used in inductions, although they are quite unnecessary. One is a spiral which rotates as the subject watches it. Another is a quite expensive, elaborate machine which is supposed to affect the brain when it is looked at, thus producing hypnosis. Actually, a stroboscopic light or vibrating effect when flashed or sounded at the rate of about fifteen a minute will almost surely produce a trance. This effect can sometimes be witnessed while driving in country districts. If the sun is shining from beyond a long hedge or row of trees, with the light coming through the trunks of the trees, it is a definite stroboscopic effect and can cause the driver to slip into hypnosis.

One of the most spectacular stage methods of induction is for the subject to stand, the operator beside him. He is swayed back and forth slightly while standing just in front of a chair. As he is swaying backward (eyes closed), the operator suddenly claps his hands together beside the subject's ear and shouts loudly the command "SLEEP!" It is most effective and the subject will probably collapse into the chair in a deep state, being assisted into the chair by the operator. This is an amusing method but certainly is not recommended.

In using the pendulum to answer questions, the subject should be watching with his attention fixed on it. In this situation he is quite likely to slip spontaneously into hypnosis, which happens frequently. Suggestions may be given then to bring greater depth. This is a method which I often use in my work.

The method of induction which is my choice and which I use perhaps about half of the time involves having the subject stand up in front of a chair. I ask him to look into my eyes and to count backward aloud from one hundred. While he is counting I will be talking to him. He is to count slowly, taking his time. While he counts I place my hands on his shoulders and move him about in a slight clockwise circle. Usually the subject starts counting in a normal tone of voice, soon his voice begins to fade off and he is counting slower. Very frequently a number is missed in the count, then another one is missed. Sometimes the subject will skip ten numbers at a time, going from seventy to fifty-nine. He is aware of this, and so am I. I see that he is slipping into hypnosis, as he may even stop counting.

While the subject counts backwards I am talking to him. I talk of how heavy his eyelids are growing, how listless he is becoming, how he is relaxing more and more. If his eyes do not close by the time he reaches the count of eighty-five, I ask him to close them.

As I move the subject around in the circle I also learn something. If he is easy to move he is not resisting and will quickly enter hypnosis. If he is hard to move in the circle, he is unconsciously resisting hypnosis, so I continue the induction talk for a longer time. The average subject will be in hypnosis by the time he has counted to seventy, which means this is a rapid method taking only a couple of minutes.

I then ask him to sit down and steer him into the chair, which is right behind him. With this technique the subject realizes that he is becoming hypnotized. After he is seated I use deepening techniques. The entire time spent with this method is seldom over four or five mintues.

There are several ways of gaining greater trance depth. One which I find very effective is to ask the subject to imagine he is standing at the top of an escalator, such as is found in some stores. He is to visualize the steps moving down in front of him, and the railing. I then count backwards from ten to zero, asking him to step on the escalator and to stand with his hand on the railing while I count, each count taking him deeper. At zero he is to step off at the bottom. Depending on the results I may have the subject go down one or more escalator levels as though going down different floors in a building.

Some women do not like to ride escalators and I make it a point to ask about this. If there is objection I suggest that they walk down a staircase instead.

The induction of any hypnotic phenomena tends to deepen the trance. If I see that the subject is in at least a medium state I will suggest a glove anesthesia of the hand nearest to me as I am sitting. This is very effective and shows the person that he is in hypnosis. Any challenging test which is successful also does this and will tend to bring a greater depth of trance.

Another deepening device which is also impressive to the patient is to suggest that his arm (right if he is right-handed, left if left-handed) will rise up to his face without his lifting it voluntarily. It will go up of its own accord. When an arm lifts without conscious volition it will almost invariably move in slight jerks, each one moving it higher. The movement is never very fast and may be very slow, requiring four or five minutes of time. If the movement is smooth and quicker, the operator should inform the subject that he is not to move it voluntarily but to let it go up of its own accord.

Of course one of the best deepening methods is the simple matter of using suggestion : "You are goir.₅ deeper and deeper, deeper and deeper, just as deep as you wish to go." The phrase "deeper and deeper" can be repeated again and again. Sometimes the operator might say to the subject, "I will say nothing at all for the next moment or two while you let yourself sink deeper and deeper, relaxing more and more."

The following is intended merely as one example of what might be said as an induction talk. In fact, the wording would be changed to fit the reactions seen in the subject, but it will serve as an example:

"Make your self comfortable, so you can relax completely. See that none of your clothing is tight. Now take a deep breath which will help you relax your muscles as you exhale. Now take another deep breath. And another. Soon you will notice that your eyelids begin to feel heavy and they may wink. They may wink more and more. They will grow heavier and heavier, heavier and heavier. You will find it harder and harder to hold them open. They are getting heavier and heavier. Your vision may become somewhat blurry. You may find it hard to swallow. The eyelids are so heavy now, so awfully heavy. Soon they will want to close. They are so heavy, so awfully heavy. [If there is no indication of this the suggestions can be further repeated.] Now you can hardly hold them open. Just let them close. You are probably feeling very listless now, very relaxed and listless, drowsy and relaxed. It is so pleasant to feel drowsy and listless. Let yourself relax still more. A feeling of well-being comes over you as if all your cares had been set aside and nothing now seems to matter. You are so listless now, so listless. Just let yourself go, drifting deeper and deeper. Deeper with each breath you take. Deeper still.

"Pay attention only to my voice. Nothing else matters and nothing will disturb you. Let yourself relax completely now. Let every muscle go loose and limp. You will notice a growing feeling of heaviness in your arms and legs, perhaps your whole body. There may be tingly feelings here and there. Your breathing is slow and easy now. You are aware and hear me but it is too much trouble to think very much. Let go completely. You are going deeper now. Deeper and deeper.

"Let your muscles relax now. Let them go loose and limp. Begin with your feet, then your lower legs and now your upper legs, right up to the hips. Let all the muscles relax. Relax your stomach and abdominal muscles. Your back, your chest muscles. Now your shoulders and neck. Then let your arms relax clear down to the finger tips. Now your facial muscles. Relax now, relax.

"I am going to lift your hand now, the hand closest to me. Let it rest on mine. Your arm and hand will lose the feeling of heaviness and will begin to get lighter and lighter. In a moment your hand will begin to float up into the air, toward your face, the arm bending at the elbow and the hand floating up without any effort on your part, all by itself. It is light now, light, light as a feather. It seems as though it wants to lift, like something is pulling it up, up towards your face. It will float up, away from my hand. Up, up. As it lifts, you will go deeper and deeper. The higher the hand goes the deeper you will go. The deeper you go, the higher the hand lifts. When your fingers touch your face, you will be very,

very deep. Soon they will touch. Up, up still higher. [The words should fit the response that is made. As soon as the hand touches the face, it can be suggested that it will go down to the former position.]

"Now you can continue to go deeper and deeper as I talk. With each breath you can go deeper. Use your imagination now. Visualize an escalator in front of you, as in some stores. You are at the top of the escalator and you can see the steps moving down in front of you, and the railing. You are all alone. It is your private escalator. I will count backwards from ten to zero and as I start to count, imagine you are stepping on the escalator. Put your hand on the railing and stand there, letting yourself go deeper and deeper as the steps take you down. Step off at the bottom at zero.

"Ten. Now step on. Nine, eight, each count takes you deeper. Seven, six, five, four, three, two. Deeper and deeper with each breath you take, one and zero. Deeper still." (Induction could be continued with challenging tests if desired.)

The operator should learn to speak slowly and in a monotone. With some practice it is even possible to set up a kind of rhythm as the talk continues.

It is very rare for there to be any difficulty in awakening a subject. Usually the operator merely suggests that he will count to three or possibly to five and that the subject will then awaken, relaxed, refreshed, and feeling wonderfully well. The operator must be careful to note if the subject is then wide awake. He should never be dismissed until the operator is sure of this. Observation will quickly tell. Most subjects awaken immediately but if the trance is a deep one it might take two, three, even five minutes for awakening to be complete.

8
Hypnosis with Children

Mention has already been made of the fact that children usually are excellent subjects. Of those between the ages six and twelve or perhaps even fourteen, 80 percent will be able to reach a deep state of hypnosis in a very short time. Induction methods and induction talks will vary with the age of the child, since it is necessary to talk on a level which a child will understand. A five-year-old might not know what the word *relax* means, but can be told to let his muscles go loose and floppy.

A rather interesting induction method with younger children is the use of a three-minute egg-timer – a miniature hour-glass. It is set so the sand is falling from the upper part after it has been explained to the child that this is very special sand obtained directly from the Sandman. As he watches the fall of the sand, he will become very sleepy; by the time all the grains have fallen he will be sound asleep, but this is a different kind of sleep because he will hear everything. Usually the child will be in a deep trance by the time all the sand has fallen into the lower part of the timer.

Almost any induction technique can be used with children, though usually the method will be abbreviated, with results coming quickly. If the child is given the impression that a game is to be played and the induction is fitted to that idea, it is very effective.

Often it is not even necessary to go through any actual induction technique with a child. Inducing some hypnotic phenomenon will act to bring on a trance state. A good example is to produce anesthesia in the child, which can usually be accomplished easily. In order to bring on the anesthesia, the child must slip into hypnosis. While anesthesia can be developed in other ways an excellent one with children is outlined here.

It is explained to the child that pain nerves work on an actual electrical impulse. It is then said that one hand is to be anesthetized. Pressure will be felt if the hand is pinched, but there will be no pain. It is explained that the pain nerves in the hand run up the child's arm, into the spine at the back of the neck, and on into his brain. He is then told to shut his eyes and imagine in his head a long row of electric light switches. Above each switch is a colored light, each turned on. Each light is a different color or shade of colors. Several can be mentioned. One particular switch and light controls the nerves in the right hand, and it is said which one does this, perhaps the light blue light. He is to turn this switch off in his imagination and see the light blue light go out. When he has done this he is to nod. It is explained that now he has cut off nerve currents to his brain and his hand will now be anesthetized. A test of this can be made by pinching the hand.

This technique was developed by a dentist who explained it to me several years ago. At that time my daughter was nine years old. One Sunday shortly after this I tried it with her. She developed anesthesia in her hand and found she had no pain on pinching the hand. Afterwards she went outside to play and in a little while came in with two other children, some of her friends.

"Look, Dad," she remarked triumphantly, "They've all got pain shut off in their hands. They can both do it."

Even a four-year-old child knows how electric lights work and how to turn off a switch, so this technique is excellent in producing anesthesia, not only with children but with adults.

Pediatricians and pedodontists who use hypnosis in practice find it of the greatest value. Most children have been hurt in visiting either doctor or dentist, even if only given a "shot." They then fear such a visit. Where hypnosis is used children lose their fears and may even welcome a visit to the physician or the dentist.

There are many illnesses and conditions suffered by children which can be treated most successfully with hypnosis. Among them is asthma, an illness which the physician seldom is able to cure, although it may be somewhat modified by use of drugs. Dr. Raymond LaScola, a pediatrician in Santa Monica, California, is one of the instructors with Hypnosis Symposiums and has treated asthmatic children with hypnosis for many years. In one or two sessions the child is usually over his asthma. He is shown while in hypnosis how he himself can control it, being able to "turn it on," or end the attack. It is most unfortunate that so few physicians know how readily asthma in children can be overcome in this way.

Hypnosis is of great value in treating many other conditions, including allergy, bed-wetting, finger-nail biting, stuttering, tics, and character disturbances.

9
Is Hypnosis Dangerous?

Undoubtedly there are some dangers involved in the use of hypnosis, but they have been greatly exaggerated. One psychiatrist has gone so far as to tour the country lecturing to medical, dental, and even lay groups on the terrible dangers of hypnosis. He collected several cases of supposed damaging factors that had occurred in some cases and cited them. Other psychiatrists, authorities on hypnosis, have commented that most of these cases are hardly good evidence because the harm caused may have had nothing to do with the fact that the subject was hypnotized. In order to make a point the conclusion was leaped at that it was hypnosis which was responsible. Here's an example:

One case cited was of a woman who was greatly overweight. A physician hypnotized her to help her lose weight, suggesting that she continue to shed the excess pounds until she was at a normal weight. She lost eighty pounds, and then committed suicide. The psychiatrist claimed this was because she had had a psychological need to be fat, and when she had lost weight and could not tolerate the situation, she had killed herself. However, he had no idea what had caused her to commit suicide, which might have had no relationship to her weight loss. In fact, if she had had such a strong need for the excess poundage, hypnotic suggestion would never have been effective and caused her to reduce.

Milton Erickson, M.D., a psychiatrist and one of the leading authorities on hypnosis, has stated that hypnosis itself has never been harmful in any way to a subject, but that like drugs or any other treatment, it can be misused. It is misuse, not hypnosis itself, which could be harmful. This is why it is foolish to be a subject for a stage hypnotist or anyone who is not well aware of possible dangers and not thoroughly competent with hypnosis.

It can safely be stated that contraindications for the use of hypnosis vary considerably with the operator and with the subject. Anyone greatly disturbed, greatly depressed, on the verge of a "nervous breakdown," or in danger of becoming insane should not be hypnotized under ordinary circumstances. Yet a psychiatrist might well use hypnosis with such a person.

Since there has been some publicity about the possible dangers and bad effects with hypnosis, they should be discussed. One criticism is that the subject becomes entirely too dependent on the operator in a theraputic situation. This is related to the rapport phenomenon. It is true that this does occur early in therapy, but as the patient makes progress his dependency diminishes, and with successful conclusion of the therapy the dependency is ended. In fact, there is dependency in any physician-patient relationship.

There are other criticisms of the use of hypnosis in psychotherapy which authorities disregard as being without merit.

One definite danger, although probably quite minor, is the matter of an operator forgetting to remove some suggestion or phenomenon which has been induced. After the subject is awakened, the condition might persist. An example would be where anesthesia had been suggested and was not removed. It is questionable how long this would continue. Undoubtedly it would depend on the individual, and perhaps the depth of hypnosis. One factor which would be important here is what has been called the "teleology" of the subconscious. Put in common language it means that the subconscious tends to protect, and will reject something harmful. This could be illustrated by an experience of my own.

Some time ago a dentist and I were on a TV program of which the producer was a mutual friend. In preparing for this the dentist was hypnotized and given the suggestion that he could smell only perfume. He was then given some perfume to smell, followed by some triple-strength ammonia, which is three times stronger than household ammonia and impossible to smell without tearing and coughing. The dentist merely remarked what a nice odor it had!

When we repeated this in front of the TV cameras, I gave the perfume and the ammonia in small bottles to the TV producer, who was on stage with us. He let the dentist smell the perfume first. Apparently a bit doubtful of the matter, he then took a strong whiff of the ammonia himself. He coughed, choked, and his eyes watered profusely. Finally he had the dentist smell it, with no reaction following.

More than a year later this dentist told me he seemed to have lost his sense of smell. He remarked that he could only smell flowers. This caused me to remember our TV show and that I had completely forgotton in the hurry and excitement of the TV show to remove the suggestion hallucinating his sense of smell. Rehypnotized and the suggestion removed, the dentist then recovered his normal sense of smell. Aside from illustrating the failure to remove a suggestion, this also illustrates the teleology of the subconscious. I am sure that the dentist's sense of smell would have returned and instantly detected the smell of smoke from a fire if one had occurred. That would have indicated danger, and the suggestion causing his loss of the sense of smell would immediately have been nullified.

Another possible danger, in that it could cause much discomfort to the patient, is age regression. In taking a subject back to any definite age or event this question should always be asked with the ideomotor answering technique: "Is it all right for you to return to this?" Whatever might have happened at that time is unknown to the operator, perhaps a very traumatic experience, perhaps an illness of some kind.

It has been mentioned that subjects almost invariably will awaken when asked to do so. In very rare instances there may be difficulty in bringing the person out of hypnosis. This can be quite embarrassing to the operator, but probably the only real danger in the situation is if the operator becomes alarmed and frightened. The subject will sense this at once, and then might well become frightened or even hysterical himself.

There is always some reason for this failure to awaken from hypnosis. The subject may know why this is happening, but more likely he does not know. The cause can be sought with the questioning technique. Usually it will be found to be unconscious association with some past experience. No one ever stayed in hypnosis for very long and if nothing were to be done the subject would probably go into normal sleep and awaken after a time. If the reason for not coming out is not discovered he probably could be awakened with no difficulty merely by having his face wiped off with a cold, wet towel.

The great French psychiatrist of the 1890's, Janet, once said, "The only danger to hypnosis is that it is not dangerous enough." David B. Cheek, M.D., of San Francisco has said, "The mechanics by which hypnosis can do harm are not different from the tools which Lady Macbeth used on her husband, which Cassius used on the honorable Brutus, which Iago used on Othello. We can do more harm with ignorance of hypnosis than we can by intelligently using the forces of suggestion."

It should be mentioned here that no report has ever been made of bad results ever being suffered with the use of self-hypnosis.

Sometimes when a person is hypnotized, his behavior will be unexpected by the operator, and may be very disconcerting. For instance, a woman subject may break into hearty crying when hypnotized. The inexpert operator's first thought with any untoward reaction would be to awaken the subject. Actually, it would be much better to suggest to the subject that she go even deeper, for he could handle the situation much better with the subject in hypnosis rather than awake, and suggesting that she go deeper is most reassuring to her. Then he can find out why she is weeping and urge her to continue to do so until she feels better and has "gotten it out of her system." Any other unexpected behavior on the part of a subject should be handled in a similar way.

10
The Practical Applications
of Hypnosis

What uses can be made of hypnosis? Undoubtedly, its foremost applications are in the areas of medicine and psychology. Potentially its greatest use would be by psychiatrists and psychologists. While many of these professional men do use hypnosis, and regard it as extremely valuable, the majority not only do not use it but know nothing about it. The field of psychoanalysis is perhaps the greatest loser here. Of the thousands of physicians of various persuasions who have taken the courses offered by Hypnosis Symposiums, only two orthodox Freudian-type analysts have attended. Both were quite shaken at what they saw and learned, and said that they must then revise some of the ideas they had accepted. There is no doubt that hypnotherapy offers a great shortcut in psychotherapy. It should be remembered that it is not a method but a tool which can be applied to any method.

One of the most important advantages of hypnosis in psychotherapy is the brevity of treatment it affords. Instead of the three hundred to five hundred hours required for orthodox analysis or the many hours involved in briefer psychiatric treatment, hypnotherapy seldom means more than a few hours of treatment. There are some cases and situations where many hours may be required but these are exceptions. Many ailments or conditions can be alleviated in ten to twenty hours, and sometimes in only two or three hours. Hypnosis is a tremendous shortcut and, financially speaking, offers a tremendous saving in cost.

In other areas of medicine one of the greatest uses of hypnosis is in obstetrics. Tens of thousands of women have been able to go through childbirth with a minimum of pain and discomfort by means of hypnosis. Every obstetrician who has used it has termed it an ideal method not only from the viewpoint of the patient, but from his own as well, making his work far easier. And, best of all, it is much easier on the baby. It is impossible to drug the mother to relieve the pains of childbirth and not at the same time drug the infant. Babies born with the mother in hypnosis will take the first breath without having to be "swatted" to start breathing, as is almost always the case if the mother has been drugged.

A Michigan obstetrician, Ralph August, is probably the leader in the field of hypnotic childbirth. Some time ago he informed me that he had had over thirty-five hundred deliveries with the mother in hypnosis. (He has written the main textbook on this subject: *Hypnosis in Obstetrics*, McGraw-Hill). Dr. Richard Clark of Los Angeles has used hypnosis for many years and his hypnotic deliveries now are well over the two thousand mark.

The obvious advantage to a women having hypnotic delivery is the escape from excessive pain. Dr. Clark has cited his own statistics on this. He has found that 25 percent of his hypnotized patients feel no pain at all. They are perfectly conscious during delivery instead of being "out" with a drug. Fifty percent of such patients feel some pain but it is quite bearable. They have been able to raise the pain threshold considerably, but not completely. Another 25 percent although in hypnosis, are not able to shut off pain and some anesthetic is required for them.

Another advantage of the use of hypnosis in this area is that a woman is in labor for a much shorter time, approximately 25 percent less hours. The baby delivered with the mother in hypnosis not only will begin to breath without stimulation but pediatricians report that such babies sleep better, cry far less, and eat better. Obstetricians find, in this connection, that they can bring on the flow of milk in the mother much quicker by hypnotic suggestion, or can shut it off if the mother prefers not to nurse her child.

Dr. Willaim Kroger, an obstetrician, has cited the following advantages he has found in hypnotic childbirth: 1. Reduction or eradication of fear in the mother, which otherwise would cause increased pain; 2. Reduction of the amount of drugs used if they are found necessary; 3. Control of uterine contractions, felt or not as the mother sees fit; 4. Decreased shock and faster recovery; 5. Lessened incidence of operative delivery; 6. Lack of undesirable post-operative complications; 7. Shortening of time in labor; 8. Raising of resistance to fatigue; 9. Minimizing exhaustion; and 10. Aid with premature delivery.

Apparently there is no medical specialty in which hypnosis cannot be helpful. In some it is more so than in others.

It might be thought that radiology would be one field where hypnosis would be useless. Actually, it can be used to relax a patient who is having X-ray photographs made. Much more important is that it can counteract most of the side effects of heavy radiation when it is used in cancer cases. Another important use is with terminal cancer patients who are in great pain. Sometimes this is great enough so drugs cannot control or modify it, or cannot be continued over a long time. Hypnotic anesthesia can be learned by these patients so they may be kept mostly free of pain during the balance of their lives. With such cases they are taught self-hypnosis and self-induced anesthesia.

The bulk of medical practice of all kinds is the treatment of psychosomatic illnesses. These are far too many to list them all, but a few of the more common ones can be mentioned — arthritis, bursitis, migraine, allergy, asthma, some skin conditions, some intestinal ailments including colitis and stomach ulcers, chronic headaches, obesity, and many others. It is the general practitioner in medicine who has the opportunity to work on the greatest variety of conditions.

Another field where hypnosis has been found of much importance is in surgery and, relatedly, in anesthesia. Surgeons find that hypnosis can be helpful in preventing or modifying post-operative shock, in preventing urine retention after surgery, in preventing post-operative nausea, and in speeding the healing of surgical wounds. Before surgery it can be of value in reassuring the patient and bringing better relaxation. When a surgical patient is in hypnosis, anesthesiologists find that only about half as much drug is required to produce anesthesia.

For surgery, hypnotic anesthesia is preferable to drug-anesthesia but it is too easy to use drugs. Also, hypnotic anesthesia sufficient for major surgery can only be produced if the subject is in a very deep trance; hence, it is of not enough value to warrant its use in most cases. It has been found valuable as a substitute for drug anesthesia when drugs are contraindicated, as is true sometimes in cardiac cases. Almost every type of operation has been performed with only hypnosis as the anesthetic, but these cases are infrequent.

During World War II there were two reported occurrences where hypnotic anesthesia was found to be of the greatest value. After the Japanese captured Singapore, the medics in one of the prison camps ran completely out of the anesthetic drugs and were given no more for some time by the Japanese. In desperation, two Australian surgeons turned to hypnosis as the anesthetic and later reported in a paper their success with it.

A surgeon who had been a prisoner of the Japanese in the Philippines has told me that the same condition developed in the camp where he was located, anesthetic drugs running out of supply. Hypnosis was also used there extensively, although no scientific report about it was ever made.

Until recently, surgeons and anesthesiologists have been quite unaware that a patient who is unconscious during surgery will continue to hear even after being given an anesthetic drug. This is not with the conscious mind but the subconscious. This is also true with any other form of unconsciousness, as from a blow or head injury, or in normal sleep. What happens during this unconscious period, or what is said, may be quite unimportant and completely ignored. On the other hand, something might happen or be said which is threatening to the patient, and be instantly registered. Dr. David B. Cheek, one of the instructors in our Hypnosis Symposium courses, first called this to the attention of his colleagues in several papers which he has written. Subsequently, this has been confirmed by several other surgeons and anesthesiologists. Most of these professional men still are ignorant of this fact, however, possibly resulting in bad effects on a patient.

Dr. L. S. Wolfe, an anesthesiologist, has written of deaths resulting during surgery by a surgeon remarking that "it's malignant" when cancer is discovered during the operation, or from some other threatening statement.

In demonstrations during our courses we have frequently been able to show that this is true. Surgical patients do hear if what is said or done has importance to them. In one course Dr. Cheek was demonstrating with one of the physicians taking the class acting as the subject. He was regressed to surgery for an appendectomy. Asked if he heard anything during the operation which was frightening or disturbing he replied verbally that he did not. At the same time with finger signalling, his forefinger was indicating "yes." With urging and suggestion he was then able to bring this into consciousness. There had been two unpleasant or disturbing comments made by the surgeon. The first was, "it's gangrenous." He was only sixteen years old at the time of the operation and did not know what the word gangrenous meant, but the way it was said sounded very ominous and he was frightened. The second remark by the surgeon was, "Let's get out of here and go home." This was said as the surgery was almost completed. The boy did not realize that this was a figure of speech and he thought they were going to go away and leave him on the operating table with his abdomen still open.

In another symposium, a surgeon who had taken a previous course and was aware that patients hear while under an anesthetic told us of one of his cases. He had performed an appendectomy on a woman patient and was just beginning to sew up the wound when the anesthetist interrupted. They talked for a moment and the anesthetist remarked to the surgeon, "You'd better finish your sewing or you may have some ruffles in there." A few days later when he removed the stitches from the wound the patient inquired, "Are there any ruffles in there?" The remark had registered in her subconscious mind and was threatening to her.

Still another interesting result of a physician's remark during surgery was the case of a prominent folk singer. His uncle, a physician, had sent him to see me because he felt sure he had lost his ability to sing well. He believed his voice was affected, and as he was making a great deal of money from his singing, this was a serious problem. His wife told me that she could see no difference in his present singing from his former singing. Ralph, as we will call him, was greatly disturbed. "My voice is gone," he remarked sadly, "I'm in a terrible spot."

With pendulum questioning it was found that his trouble went back to a tonsillectomy operation three months earlier. Some idea had been picked up at that time, during the operation, about his singing. Under hypnosis he was regressed to the operation. He told of being wheeled into the operating room, receiving an injection of a drug (sodium pentothal) in one arm and of then becomming unconscious. Apparently nothing disturbing had occured until the operation was completed, when he reported hearing the surgeon saying to the anesthesiologist, "Well, that takes care of this yowler and his voice." Apparently, the surgeon was not exactly an enthusiast to folk singing!

After being awakened, Ralph told of his fears about the operation. Would it affect his voice in any way? Could he sing as well afterwards? The operation was imperative, but he was very fearful of its results. He had asked the surgeon whether his voice would be affected and had received a very noncommital reply, which only added to his fear. The remark made by the surgeon at the end of the operation confirmed his fears, though he had completely misinterpreted it. The surgeon had obviously only meant that the operation was over and that his voice would be unaffected — "taken care of." His fear caused him to think the worst, that he could only "yowl" now.

I had great difficulty in subsequent sessions convincing Ralph that this was what was meant by the surgeon's remark. He was very skeptical and still sure that his voice was ruined. I was unable to convince him otherwise, but suggested that he sing for other professionals and learn what they said about his voice now in comparison to what it had been in past recordings. This was successful in changing his views, as he continued his career and reached even greater success in folk singing.

A field of medicine where hypnosis may be of value but which has been almost unexplored is diagnosis. Those who are familiar with hypnosis quickly learn to have great respect for the abilities and powers of the subconscious mind. It would seem that this part of the mind might very well know what particular organ in the body was affected in a disease and could give this information with the questioning technique. In the case of an infection, it could hardly say what "bug" was responsible, but might know the areas affected.

My own one experience in this area was when a girl patient of mine complained one day of suffering considerable pelvic pain. I urged her to see her gynecologist, which she did, on the basis that it might be a tubal pregnancy or something else which would need attention. When I saw her two days later she was in greater pain but said the physician had told her after examination that there was no tubal pregnancy or anything else wrong which he could detect. She asked if her subconscious mind would know if there might be a tubal pregnancy and I informed her that I didn't know but we could ask. With the pendulum questioning, the reply was that she did have such a pregnancy. The gynecologist, on more thorough examination, found that was indeed the case.

Hypnosis has valuable applications in dentistry and today many dentists are trained in hypnodontia. Perhaps its greatest professional acceptance by the dental profession in one locality is where I am living. Out of a total of eighty dentists in this area, thirty-three have taken courses in the use of hypnosis and I believe all are using it in their practice. This is a bit more than 40 percent. Nationwide, it is doubtful if more than 5 percent use it, but some can be found in every city and in many smaller towns.

It can be shown through hypnotic suggestion that the subconscious mind can affect the action of some organs and glands, including circulation. It would seem that this inner part of the mind controls the entire physical mechanism of the body. The applications of hypnosis are largely unknown in respect to these physical controls. It would seem that some entirely physical ailments could be treated successfully or at least modified. Let's consider one such situation where results are known: the removal of warts. Warts are a cellular growth with a virus present. Hypnotic suggestion can usually cause warts to fade away and be gone within about ten days. What is involved is not known, but they are removed.

There are still other uses of hypnosis which are covered in later chapters, including applications of self-hypnosis for insomnia, weight reduction, stopping smoking, improving studying, and improving sports.

11
Self-Hypnosis

For most purposes the applications of hypnosis are best accomplished by being hypnotized and treated by someone who is proficient and is a professional – a physician, psychologist, or dentist. Your nearest medical association office may be able to refer you to such a person for there usually is someone in the area who is experienced. If you should be unable to locate a qualified person I will try to refer you to someone, provided that you write me enclosing a stamped self-addressed envelope for reply.

There are some situations where it is possible to accomplish much by means of self-hypnosis, something most people can learn, although no statistics on this are available. Undoubtedly the best way to learn self-hypnosis is to have someone else hypnotize you and give you post-hypnotic suggestions to enter hypnosis when you go through some brief formula.

However, it is usually possible to learn self-hypnosis by following the methods which will be given to you here. If you find you are not too successful with these methods you might have some friend read the induction talk which is in the next chapter. An alternative would be to make a tape recording of this induction talk and play it while you listen. Most readers will be able to learn auto-hypnosis without help. It is largely a matter of following instructions and practicing a few times. It is a learning process. Practice improves your ability and you probably will go a little deeper with each practice session.

The real secret of getting into hypnosis is fixation of attention, with relaxation and "letting go." Avoid trying, for it must come of itself and trying tends to hold one back, especially if you are doubtful of success. In that situation you may encounter the Law of Reversed Effect, which has been explained in a previous chapter.

Until you have obtained some proficiency with induction it is best to use some object for eye fixation, to hold your attention. This can be almost anything, preferably some bright object. It can be a picture on the wall, a spot, a doorknob. Perhaps one of the best objects is a lighted candle. The flickering flame seems to help. It should be in a candle stick or fixed so you do not worry about it falling over and it should be placed in a position where you can view it without straining. The plastic pendulum used in obtaining ideomotor responses to questions also makes a very good object for fixation.

You should take a comfortable position, which can be sitting up or lying down. Be sure your clothing is not so tight so it would cause discomfort. Select a time and situation so you will not be interrupted. A good time to practice is when you go to bed at night.

To help with relaxation take two or three deep breaths and let yourself go as much as possible. Continue to keep your gaze fixed on whatever object you select. Three or four minutes is enough for this. Then close your eyes and take another deep breath.

In practicing allow at least fifteen minutes for the session. There is a tendency up to a certain point to continue to slip deeper into hypnosis the longer you are in that state. It is not necessary to say anything aloud for self-induction. You merely think. Select a key word or phrase which is to be a signal for you to enter hypnosis. A good phrase is *relax now*. The first word is a suggestion, the second is a different suggestion meaning at once. This word or phrase should be repeated slowly three times.

The next step is to let go and relax as much as possible. Thinking of various muscle groups will help. Begin at your toes and work up to your hip, one leg at a time. First make the muscles in any group as taut as possible, then suddenly let them go loose and limp. After relaxing the legs, think of your stomach and abdominal muscles and let them loosen up. Follow progressively with your chest and breathing muscles, your back muscles, the shoulders and neck. Then let one arm relax from the shoulders down to the fingertips; then the other arm. Finally let your facial muscles relax. Relaxation of your whole body will help you enter hypnosis and even deepen it. You will find as you go deeper that this relaxation process continues spontaneously. People often say they achieve a greater degree of relaxation under hypnosis than they have ever known before.

After repeating your key word or phrase and having gone through this relaxation process, you should be at least lightly in hypnosis. In order to reach a deeper stage, suggestions will help. Think to yourself, repeating it several times, "I am now going deeper and deeper."

Visual imagery is also effective in reaching a deeper stage. Imagine yourself standing at the top of an escalator. See the steps moving down in front of you, and the escalator railings. Now count backwards from twenty to zero, at the same time in your imagination stepping on the escalator and standing with your hand on the railing. The steps move down carrying you with them deeper and deeper into hypnosis. When you reach zero in the count, imagine yourself stepping off at the bottom.

In your early practice session this escalator technique can be repeated two or three times as though going down different levels. Once you gain proficiency one is enough. You may then count only from ten instead of twenty. If you prefer, you could imagine an elevator or staircase instead of this escalator for this method of deepening hypnosis.

All of this takes only a few moments. Follow it by letting your thoughts go to anything pleasant, using further visual imagery. Imagine yourself on a fishing trip, lying on a beach, in a boat, walking through a woods, perhaps reviewing some former pleasant experience or imagining some trip you would like to take.

With self-hypnosis there sometimes is a tendency to drop off into normal sleep, this being more apt to occur if you are tired. You can prevent this by suggestions to yourself that you will stay in hypnosis until ready to awaken, saying this as soon as you finish the escalator technique.

While in hypnosis your sense of time may be somewhat distorted and you may find a half-hour or more has passed, although it has only seemed like a few minutes. You can give yourself a suggestion that you will awaken spontaneously at some given time or after the elapse of some definite period of time, such as twenty minutes.

Awakening yourself is merely a matter of deciding to awaken, counting slowly to three with the thought that you are now about to awaken. You will then be fully awake and alert. It is well also to suggest that you will be completely relaxed, will feel very refreshed and clear-headed when you awaken. Since hypnosis is not sleep, using the word "awaken" for emergence from hypnosis is not too appropriate but most operators use it as a matter of convenience and for lack of a better word.

Becoming proficient with self-hypnosis is a learning process and takes practice. Some will enter a very deep state at the first induction attempt. If this occurs, you will undoubtedly be aware of being deeply hypnotized. Unless it happens, you may wonder at first if you are having any result. Pay no attention to results in the first three or four sessions, taking it for granted that you are in at least a light state. Subjects almost invariably consciously underestimate the depth reached, until they become more experienced.

Unless you are sure you are reaching a good depth in early attempts, make no tests until after your fourth session. One good test is called *arm levitation*. In this you suggest that one arm will begin to lose all sensation of weight, will become lighter and lighter until the hand begins to float up toward your face with no voluntary effort. It is to lift of its own accord. Keep repeating this suggestion and note that you have not stated which arm it will be that will lift. Very soon you will notice the difference in weight in one arm and it soon will begin to move. Perhaps at first it will be the fingers, or perhaps the whole hand, and then the whole arm. The motion will be quite slow and if the movement is involuntary there will be slight jerky movements of the arm as it lifts. Suggest that the motion will continue until your fingers touch your face. The movement may be smoother and faster as the hand nears the face. When you have felt your fingers make a contact somewhere on your face, let your arm go down again into any comfortable position.

Another test you can make is to suggest that one arm is becoming very heavy, that it is getting heavier and heavier and will soon be so heavy that it would be impossible to lift such a heavy weight. Keep repeating this idea until you are aware of great heaviness. Then suggest that you cannot possibly lift it, repeating this several times. Say that the harder you try, the heavier the arm will be and that it cannot be lifted. (You are invoking that Law of Reversed Effect.) Then make an effort, but you will find that the lifting muscles seem to be paralyzed and will not function. After making an effort, remove the suggestion of heaviness, saying that now the weight of the arm will return to normal and that it could be lifted readily.

Still another good test is *eye catalepsy* — inability to open the eyelids. Counting often helps in making such tests. Suggest that your eyelids are becoming heavy and that it will be impossible to open them. When you have counted to three they will be locked together tightly and cannot be opened. Wording of the suggestions could be like this: "When I've counted to three I'll be unable to open my eyes. The harder I try the tighter they will stick together. ONE, my eyelids are glueing fast together. TWO, it's as though the lids were welded into one piece and I couldn't possibly open them. THREE, now they are locked together, locked tightly together. They are tight, tight, tight." As you keep repeating the word "tight" try to open them but stop trying as soon as you find you cannot do so.

Sometimes such tests will fail, which could indicate that you are not in hypnosis, or possibly skepticism may counteract your suggestions even though you may be hypnotized. A test can fail even if you are in hypnosis.

As has been mentioned, depth of hypnosis will vary. At one moment you may be lighter than at another, or perhaps you may be deeper. You may even notice that there is a kind of wave pattern present, where you tend to come up on the crest, lighter in depth, then sink into the trough, going deeper. This is more likely to be apparent in the deeper stages.

In your first practice sessions make no attempt to test or to try to find the depth you have reached. After the fourth session you can use the imaginary yardstick method of determining depth. By this time you should be reaching a greater depth than in your first sessions. When you have practiced eight or ten times you probably will be reaching a depth as great as you can reach. Sometimes there are subconscious blocks working to prevent you from reaching greater depths. These can often be removed and then you can reach greater depths. Possible blocks will be considered in the chapter on resistances.

When you are utilizing self-hypnosis, there are some situations where you must be able to open your eyes and stay in hypnosis. Hypnosis is not sleep and yet there may be some unconscious association of hypnosis with sleep. Sometimes opening the eyes will cause a subject to come out of hypnosis, or will lighten the depth. Suggestions to yourself can prevent this. Of course you can be hypnotized without ever closing your eyes, as happens often with spontaneous states of hypnosis. An operator usually likes to have a subject close his eyes because it shuts out distractions and makes induction easier. This is also true with self-hypnosis.

It is quite possible to open your eyes and stay in

hypnosis even if you are only in a light state, but it is much more likely if you are at a depth of fifteen inches or more on our yardstick. In learning to open your eyes there should be no attempt until you reach such a depth, or if you can only achieve a light state. It should be impressed on your subconscious that you can open your eyes and remain in hypnosis. Suggestions for this could be as follows:

"I am going to open my eyes and will remain deeply hypnotized. Whether my eyes are open or closed need not affect the depth of hypnosis I am in. As I open my eyes I will go even deeper. I will go still deeper as my eyes are opened. Of course my vision will be perfectly normal."

There is a tendency to go deeper into hypnosis with any successful test or with any phenomenon produced. Therefore when you are sure you can reach a depth of at least fifteen inches, you can begin inducing and experiencing some of the other phenomena. You might begin with hypnotic anesthesia which usually is easily induced. Being able to shut off pain can be valuable at times, as when visiting your dentist for instance.

Various techniques can be employed to produce anesthesia. If you can reach twenty inches or more in depth on your yardstick, you can suggest that your hand will become anesthetized when you have stroked it three times with the other hand; that it will then become insensitive, numb, and that you will feel no pain if it is stimulated. A suitable test is merely to pinch the skin hard with the fingers of the other hand. In testing in this way you will be aware of pressure but it will not hurt. You do feel pressure but pain is inhibited.

At lighter depths the technique of developing anesthesia by use of the imagined light switches can be applied. You can make your own decision as to what part of the body is controlled by which switch with its colored light. For instance you might tell yourself that the switch with the light blue light above it is in control of the area of the upper jaw; the dark blue light and switch control the nerves in the lower jaw.

In developing anesthesia in some painful area it is best first to induce it in some other region, your dominant hand probably being the most suitable. Let us say that the light green light switch goes to that hand. Imagine you are turning off that switch and see the light green light above it go out. Suggest to yourself that all the nerve current to that hand is now cut off and the hand will become completely anesthetized, numb and lifeless.

Wait a moment and let the numbness develop. When it feels quite numb, test by pinching, lightly at first and then very hard, using your finger nails. You may have developed complete anesthesia or may find that there is a little pain experienced. You may have raised the pain threshold considerably and yet not have completely eliminated the sensation of pain. Make a comparison by pinching the unanesthetized hand. With practice you should be able to induce complete anesthesia, though sometimes a partial one is all that can be produced.

Always remember to remove the anesthesia by turning on the switch and seeing the light above it come on again. If it is desirable, anesthesia can be maintained for several days, but a definite time to terminate it should be set. Of course common sense must be used in determining when hypnotic anesthesia should be used. In case of an injury or pain from an illness are you justified in removing the anesthesia? First the cause should certainly be learned. A pain in the abdomen might be because of an attack of appendicitis. If anesthesia were to be induced, it might mask the breaking of the appendix, a very dangerous situation. It is well to use with a sprained ankle, but harmful with a broken ankle.

Learning to age regress (the partial type) can sometimes help to eliminate the block. It is possible to return to almost any experience in your life and relive it, unless it is one which has been repressed as frightening, unpleasant, or traumatic. Before regressing to any experience you should use the ideomotor questioning technique to learn from your inner mind if it is all right to go back to the experience.

In order to learn to regress in this way, practice by going back to some recent happening of no significance. While you would have conscious memory of such an event, you intend to relive it rather than merely remember it.

As an example, suppose you regress yourself to a recent meal at which someone else was present. Suggest that you are going back in time to the moment when you sat down to this meal. Word it like this, "I'm going back in time to last night, to the moment when I sat down to dinner. Now I am drifting back in time, drifting back a few hours. Now it is last night as I sat down to dinner. The scene is clearing. I will see it clearly and vividly."

Feel the seat under you and sense your position. In your mind's eye see the table in front of you, the dishes, and the food on the plate. Visualize all these things. If you had coffee to drink, go to the moment when you drank it. Feel the cup in your fingers as you lift it. See the brown color of the coffee, smell the aroma, taste it, and feel the warmth.

Then go to some moment when you heard someone speak. Look at the person and see how the person is dressed, the color and pattern of her clothing if it is a woman, the color of his suit and of his necktie if it is a man. If things are a bit vague, suggest again that the scene is to become clearer and more vivid. Hear the conversation now. Hear the voice or voices. In this way you are developing recall with all five of the senses and it is much more than mere remembering.

When you can regress to a recent event such as this one, practice returning to some interesting childhood experience at some age between 4 and 6. Select a trip to the zoo, a Christmas or a birthday. Be indefinite as to the year and let your subconscious select the exact time and experience. Probably you will find yourself seeing some scene, as you did as a child. Try to develop it and make it vivid.

With the methods given here you should, in all probability, be able to hypnotize yourself. However, you may not have the success you would like. In this event, make a tape recording of the induction talk given in the next chapter. Play it while you listen, or you can have a friend read it to you. Or, as was stated, if this is not successful, visit a professional man, a physician or psychologist familiar with hypnosis who can help you, asking him to teach you self-hypnosis. Two or three sessions is usually sufficient for this and the cost should be moderate.

There are a great many applications of self-hypnosis which can be of great value to a person who has learned it. In some of the succeeding chapters these applications will be considered. However it should always be remembered that treatment by a competent therapist would be most beneficial in the majority of these situations.

Of course the benefits possible and the uses will vary considerably with the individual who uses self-hypnosis.

Some can never reach more than a light state while still others can induce a somnambulistic trance. For most purposes it can be said that a medium depth is probably ideal, as there is such a lethargy in deeper stages. Self-hypnosis can even be very effective if only a light state is reached.

A woman psychologist was to give a speech on hypnosis to a rather large audience which would include many psychologists. I had taught her self-hypnosis some time before, and she had become very proficient, able to reach a very deep state. I suggested to her that it might be interesting to her listeners if she gave her talk while in self-hypnosis. Under hypnosis I gave her suggestions that she would be alert, and would give no signs of being in hypnosis in giving her talk. She even read some of the speech she had prepared, for the practice.

At the meeting I introduced her and she laid her carefully prepared speech on the table in front of her. Then she gave an entirely extemporaneous, unrehearsed talk, a very good one, completely ignoring her prepared speech. In concluding, she asked her audience if anyone had noticed that she was in hypnosis all through her talk, and still was self-hypnotized? Only two in the audience held up their hands. She then awakened herself and remarked to me that she wondered why she had not used her speech. The only reason I could think of was that her inner mind wanted her to demonstrate how well she could speak while in hypnosis but without preparing for it.

12
Inducing Self-Hypnosis

If you record the following wording you may use your own voice or have someone else read it, as you prefer. The words should be spoken slowly in a monotone. Before making a recording read the passage over once or twice. Each time you hear it you should be able to increase the trance depth until you become a good subject. Many persons will find themselves reaching a good depth the first time it is heard.

While listening you should avoid being analytic or curious about the results. Relax and let go as much as possible. Concentrate on what is said. You can shut out outside sounds or noises that might be distracting. Pay attention only to the voice as you listen.

Here is the wording:

"Make yourself comfortable, being sure your clothing is loose. It makes no difference whether you sit up or lie down, as long as you are in a comfortable position. Fix your gaze on something. While you watch it, let your eyes go out of focus if you can. Now take a deep breath. That helps you relax. The more you relax the easier it is for you to slip into hypnosis. Soon you will find you are more relaxed than you probably ever have been before. Just relax and let go.

"Soon your eyelids will being to feel rather heavy. As you continue to look at the object you've selected, the eyelids will get heavier and heavier, heavier and heavier. Probably you will begin to blink a bit. There may be a slight watering of your eyes as the eye muscles relax more and more. The lids are getting heavier and heavier. Let them wink if they seem to want to wink. Let them close whenever they want to close. The lids are relaxing more and more, which is why they feel so heavy and want to wink. Soon they will want to close. The lids are relaxing more and more. Soon they will want to close. Let them close whenever you want to. They are so heavy. Getting still heavier. It's even hard to keep them open.

"Take another deep breath now. Let your eyes close if they are not already closed. In a moment you may find that you need to swallow. Swallow whenever you feel the need.

"Probably you are developing a listless, drowsy feeling. Drowsy and rather sleepy. Very drowsy, and you feel more and more drowsy as you relax still more. You can relax more now. Begin with your right leg. Make all the muscles taut. Wiggle the toes, stretch the muscles in your calf and upper leg by moving your foot. Then let the muscles loosen up and go limp from your toes right up to your hip. Now do the same with your left leg, tightening all the muscles, then letting them go loose. Relax the whole leg from the toes to the hip.

"Your body can relax more now. Let your stomach and abdominal muscles loosen. Then your chest and breathing muscles. The muscles of your back can loosen and be limp. Let them loosen completely. Now your shoulders and the neck muscles. Often we have tension in that area. Feel the tension going out of those muscles as they loosen. And now make your right arm stiff and rigid, then let it go completely relaxed. Let all the muscles go slack from your shoulder right down to your fingertips. Your arm will relax completely. In the same way relax your left arm. Even your facial muscles will relax. Notice how comfortable you feel. All tension is leaving you, draining away. You are so very comfortable and drowsy now.

"You will listen attentively to what is being said. If there are outside noises you need pay no attention to them. They go in one ear and out the other. They are unimportant. Listen only to my voice.

"Often there is a flickering of the eyelids when you are in hypnosis. It is one of the signs of hypnosis. Sometimes they do not flicker even if you are in hypnosis. If yours do, they will soon relax and stop fluttering as you sink deeper and deeper.

"Take still another deep breath and let yourself go completely. Enjoying the dreamy, drowsy feeling. Hypnosis is not sleep, for you are always fully aware. But you will feel so very drowsy. Such a comfortable pleasant listlessness is creeping over you more and more as you relax so completely. Perhaps your whole body feels heavy, particularly your arms and legs. Notice that your breathing has changed. You are breathing more from the bottom of your lungs, abdominal breathing, and you are breathing more slowly.

"Notice the feeling of comfort and well-being which has come over you. Give way to the listless drowsiness. Everyone enjoys being in hypnosis. It is so comfortable and pleasant.

Your whole body is relaxed and tensions seem to drain away.

"Now you can go still deeper into this pleasant state. Let go and go deeper and deeper with each breath. Deeper and deeper. The deeper you go the more comfortable and pleasant it seems. Now imagine that you are standing at the top of an escalator such as are in some stores. See the steps moving down in front of you and see the railings. If you do not like to ride escalators, imagine a staircase instead. I will count backwards from ten to zero. If you are using the escalator, step on it as I begin to count, standing with your hand on the railing. Or if you use the staircase, start walking slowly down it as I count. You are all alone. It is your private escalator. When we reach zero, imagine you have reached the bottom and step off.

"*Ten* — and you step on. Each count will take you deeper and deeper. *Nine* (slowly), *eight, seven, six.* You are going deeper and deeper. *Five, four, three,* still deeper. *Two, one,* and *zero* Now, step off the escalator or staircase. You can continue to go deeper with each breath you take.

"Your arms and legs may feel guite heavy by now. They are so completely relaxed. But one of your arms is going to begin to lose any feeling of heaviness and will grow lighter and lighter. It's as if all the weight were draining out of it. It may be your right arm, or it may be the left. Let's see which one it will be. Soon the one which is getting lighter will start to lift from its position. It's getting lighter and lighter. You may feel the fingers of the hand beginning to move a little, or the whole hand may lift. The hand will start to lift, to float up towards your face, but of its own accord, without conscious effort. It goes up by itself. The hand and arm are becoming still lighter. Lighter and lighter. The hand is beginning to float up. Up toward your face. The arm starts to bend at the elbow and lift.

"It might be interesting to think of some part of your

face where you want the fingers to touch when they reach your face. It could be your forehead, your ear, your chin – any part. But your subconscious mind will see that the fingers touch some different part of your face from the one you selected. Where will it touch? It is lifting higher and higher still. It is as light as a feather. Lifting. It can move a bit faster now. If it has not yet started, lift it a few inches to give it a start and it then will continue to move up of its own accord.

"Your hand is lifting higher and higher. As it goes up you can go still deeper. The higher your hand goes, the deeper you will go. The deeper you go, the higher your hand will lift. Soon the fingers will be making a contact, touching your face at some different place from the one you consciously selected. Reaching out now to touch your face. The wrist turning. The hand goes still higher. If your hand has not already touched, it will continue to rise while we speak of other things, continuing to go up until you feel it touch your face. Then the arm will go down to some comfortable position. If it has touched you may lower it.

"Let yourself go still deeper now. How comfortable you are. Drift still deeper and enjoy it. Deeper and deeper."

You wish to learn self–hypnosis. As a matter of fact all hypnosis is really self-hypnosis. The operator is only a guide; the subject is the one who does it. You can quickly learn to be able to hypnotize yourself, just as you have spontaneously slipped into hypnosis many times.

To learn self-hypnosis you will have a formula to follow, certain things to do which will cause you to go into hypnosis. First select some key word to phrase which will be the signal for you to slip into hypnosis when you think or say the word. But it will be effective only when you intentionally say it and wish to be in hypnosis. It will have no effect except when you use it for that purpose. A good phrase is "relax now," but select any word or phrase that you prefer to use.

To hypnotize yourself take any comfortable position. You need not speak aloud, merely think the suggestions you will give yourself. Fix your gaze on something. Gaze at it intently for a moment or two, no more than three or four. Let your eyes go out of focus as you do so. Suggest to yourself that your eyelids are becoming heavier and heavier. Then let them close and say to yourself, "Now I'm going into hypnosis." Take two or three deep breaths. Then repeat your key word or phrase three times, very slowly. As you repeat it, you'll be drifting into hypnosis.

You will want to go as deeply as possible. When you have repeated your key, take another deep breath and suggest, "Now I'm going deeper." Use the imaginary escalator or staircase, while you yourself count backwards from ten to zero, including the zero. As you do this you will sink deeper. Some people find it hard to visualize. If that is true with you, just the counting backwards will take you deeper. Each time you use the backward count it will cause you to go deeper.

The first four times you practice inducing self-hypnosis, go down another level while you count again, even a third level. Each time it will take you deeper. With practice you will then need to do this only once.

After you've practiced self-induction four times, or even less if you find you are very successful, you can begin using it.

When you are ready to awaken from self-hypnosis all you need do is give yourself the suggestion, "Now I'm going to wake up." Then count slowly to three. You will then be wide awake. You will always awaken feeling relaxed, refreshed, and clear-headed.

If at any time when you are in hypnosis there should be any reason for you to awaken at once, you will awaken instantly. If the phone rings you should answer it. If there is a real danger such as a fire, you will awaken instantly and be completely alert. This would happen without this suggestion, for your subconscious mind would awaken you if there was danger of any kind.

When you have practiced four times, or if you are having good results sooner, you will be ready to open your eyes and to stay in hypnosis. There are times and conditions where you may wish to have your eyes open. Opening your eyes need not cause you to awaken. Instead, as you open your eyes you can slip even deeper into hypnosis. You can open your eyes and remain deeply in hypnosis. Your vision will be no different.

At each playing of this recording, or if you hear these words spoken to you, you will be able to go deeper into hypnosis until you have learned it well.

"Now I will count to three and you will then be completely awake and alert. Wide awake. *One,* you are beginning to awaken. *Two,* you are almost awake now. *Three,* now you are wide awake and normal in every way. You feel wonderfully well. You are wide awake now. And hasn't this been a pleasant experience? Now you will be able to hypnotize yourself at any time."

As you become interested in hypnosis and make progress in its use, you may be tempted to try to hypnotize some of your friends, or members of your family. This is not advisable. In all probability there would be no bad reactions but you are not able to judge if a person is disturbed or when hypnosis might be contraindicated. Don't become a "parlor hypnotist." Hypnosis is not a toy, though self-hypnosis is quite safe.

13
Self-Hypnosis
for Psychosomatic Conditions

Physicians have found that at least half of all illnesses have some psychological or emotional background and they are then termed psychosomatic. Some estimates are much higher in percentage. Stress can lower our resistances so that we are more susceptible to even infectious diseases. At one time or another most of us suffer from some psychosomatic ailment. Having learned self-hypnosis, one of its advantages is that it can be of help in coping with these illnesses. Of course it is only good common sense to seek medical treatment for any illness. The combination of drugs and psychotherapy may be the best treatment.

Can self-help be successful in such conditions? Not always, by any means, but frequently it can be of value, because these conditions can be more easily terminated with knowledge of their causes. Drugs treat only the symptom. In but few instances do they affect the causes. Psychotherapeutic treatment by a competent therapist is often necessary, but sometimes the causes are on a very superficial level and can be uncovered readily with the methods given here. Even when a condition is of long standing and medical treatment has been without result, sometimes these methods can give relief.

What illnesses are classed as psychosomatic? It covers most of the medical list of diseases, but here only some of the most prevalent will be considered. The condition itself may be physical; it is the causes which are psychological or emotional.

In the field of gynecological conditions usually most of them can be so classified. Menstrual disorders, especially menstrual cramps, infertility, frigidity and miscarriage are common difficulties.

With men, in the sexual area, impotence, prematureness, and infertility are almost invariably psychosomatic.

Many of the illnesses affecting the respiratory tract have such a background though not always are they psychosomatic. Colds, sinusitis, asthma, bronchitis, emphysema and tuberculosis may have psychological factors as causes. In some there may be allergic complications as well, but, in allergy, there usually are also psychological factors.

In the digestive system, peptic ulcer, colitis, constipation, vomiting (including the vomiting of pregnancy) and lack of appetite come under this heading.

Some of the conditions in the urinary systems are bed-wetting, urinary retention, incontinence, and nervous frequency.

Skeletal and muscular conditions are muscle spasm, backache, slipped disc, sciatica, bursitis, arthritis, wry neck, and headache including those of migraine type. Besides these classifications there are many other conditions — diabetes, neuralgia, hypertension, tics, some heart conditions.

In addition to psychosomatic diseases, hypnotherapy is of utmost value in many mental conditions. Various forms of neurosis such as phobias, anxiety states, hysteria, obsessions and compulsions can be treated in far less time with hypnosis than with more orthodox methods of psychotherapy. Even the more severe forms of mental disturbance termed the psychoses sometimes respond to hypnotherapy. Some forms of epilepsy, alcoholism and drug addiction can be included in the above listing.

It should be remembered that hypnosis is not a method of treatment but is a tool which can be utilized with any form of treatment, including orthodox psychoanalysis.

Successful self-treatment is more likely to be possible when the causes of any specific condition are on a superficial basis. Certainly a physician should be consulted and his advice followed. In making a diagnosis he can inform you if an ailment may have a psychological or emotional background. Many of the conditions listed here can be helpfully treated with self-hypnosis through the methods given here. On the other hand, a competent psychotherapist should always be consulted if results are lacking.

More and more physicians are becoming psychologically oriented and realize that medical treatment alone may fail to cure psychosomatic diseases. However, it is well to realize that there are still many doctors who have had no training along this line and tend to ignore psychological factors as involved.

There are some contraindications for self-treatment and for the use of self-hypnosis. Anyone who is extremely disturbed mentally, who is very depressed, who is extremely anxious, should avoid attempting self-help. There are also certain precautions which should be followed. Never attempt age regression without first learning through questioning if it is safe for you to return to some specific experience in the past. If an affirmative answer is given, there is no danger of becoming emotionally overwhelmed, if you ask the question is it safe. Another precaution should be used, again through questioning, when trying to learn of any cause which the answers determine is involved in a condition. Ask if it is all right for you to know this cause. Knowledge of the reason for some condition, as well as some past experience, can sometimes be too threatening or too overwhelming to be brought to consciousness.

You would seldom find such circumstances, for they are rare, but there is always a faint possibility of becoming too emotionally upset at something you uncover. I might add that I have never heard of anyone having had bad results from using self-help methods, even when these precautions are not taken. The inner mind seems to protect you from gaining insight which could be dangerous to know.

Freud advanced a theory that every child develops sexual feelings for the parent of the opposite sex. Undoubtedly this is sometimes a fact, but most therapists feel that this is a great exaggeration. One of my patients was a young woman with a strong anxiety neurosis, often having attacks of extreme panic. Some of her remarks and interpreting some of her dreams soon indicated that this resulted from such feelings for her father. She said, "I wonder why I can't stand to have my father touch me. I'm very fond of him." During a session with her I inadvertently and mistakenly tried to reassure her and told her that I now saw what was behind her anxiety and that we would soon have it straightened out. I never saw her again. Insight into this was intolerable and she protected herself by never returning for further treatment. In time she could have been brought to see her conflict and tolerate it, but she was not ready to know.

In order to overcome any psychosomatic ailment on your own, the first step should be to determine with questioning if there is some emotional or psychological factor involved. Wording of the question should be if there is one or more such factors. The literal answer would be "no" if you asked if there was "a" factor (one). If any are present, the inner mind certainly is aware of them.

The next step is to find the causes through questioning. There are seven key factors to look for. Only one may be in operation, more often two or three will be located, and it is even possible, though rare, for all seven to have a role. Some of the seven have been mentioned previously. These are identification, imprints, and self-punishment or masochism. Any of these are frequently present as causes. It is not necessary to describe them further.

Conflict is commonly involved, not only in psychosomatic illness, but also in the neuroses and other mental conditions. Essentially conflict arises from something we would like to do but it encounters inhibitions – "I want" running head on into "You can't." From earliest infancy our wishes are often thwarted by the dictates of parents or of society, morals and customs. One of the leading sources of conflict is sex, but there can be many other sources and kinds of conflict.

A conflict may lie deeply buried in the subconscious

and difficult to resolve because it is unrecognized. It may then bring nervous tension, anxiety, or other symptoms. When a conflict is recognized, it is easier to accept it, put up with it, or resolve it in some way.

What *motivation* can there be which would cause some symptom to develop? What purpose does the condition serve? Most everyone likes to receive sympathy and attention and sometimes an illness brings these desirable attitudes from those close to us. Motives may not be as simple as this. A common motive is self-punishment, particularly if a symptom is painful as in arthritis or headache, for instance.

Symptoms present in the neurotic condition termed hysteria usually have some motivation causing them. Hysterical paralysis of a limb could be a means of preventing the person from hitting out at something or from using the limb in some other unacceptable manner. Hysterical blindness can serve to keep the victim from seeing something that should not be seen, or as a punishment for having seen something about which he feels guilty.

One of my cases was a school-teacher who had to stop teaching because she had lost her voice - aphonia is the term for the condition. She could only speak in a faint whisper, and the ailment had persisted for almost three months. Doctors had been unable to find any physical reason for it.

The questioning technique soon located the reason why she had lost her voice. She lived with another teacher whom she had grown to dislike intently. Their lease on their apartment had another two months to run. She longed to tell her friend off, to berate her, and tell her what she thought of her and her actions. On the other hand, my teacher patient was kindly, did not want to hurt the other woman, and felt she could not financially afford to leave. She was always afraid she would lose her temper and sound off. Losing her voice was the solution. She could only talk in a whisper, which prevented her from saying the things she would like to say.

Of course the obvious answer to this conflict was to move out at once, even though she would have to pay her share of the rent for two months. Doctor bills had amounted to much more than this already. She found she could speak in a normal tone while in hypnosis and decided to go home and tell her friend she was moving as soon as she could find another apartment. On awakening, she could speak normally and had no further trouble. In this case there was not only motivation causing her to lose her voice. There was also conflict over her environmental situation.

With *organ language* we enter the field of semantics, the effect of words on us. In speaking about something unpleasant, a number of phrases are commonly used. Some examples are, "That's a headache to me," "That makes me sick," "It makes me sick at the the stomach" or "I can't stomach that," "It's a pain in the neck," "I can't swallow that," "It's a load on my chest." There are many others in fairly common usage.

The inner mind may translate the idea expressed in one of these phrases into the actual physical condition. Headaches, nausea, pain, difficulty in swallowing may follow. The person who is carrying out such an idea has no realization of the reason for his symptom. Often it will be noted that he uses this phrase in his speech.

Torticolis or wry neck is not a very common ailment and most doctors regard it as physical, from muscle tension and spasms. Few would think of it as having possible psychological causes. Mrs. Peters, a married woman with two children, visited me with this condition, having been referred by her physician who had been unable to help her. Being familiar with our questioning technique, he had asked if there was any psychological cause for the condition and the answer had been affirmative.

Wry neck usually is a condition where the head is turned to one side, pulled there by the neck muscles, and then cannot be straightened. In Mrs. Peters' case it was different. Her head was pulled down instead of to one side. Her chin rested against her neck. The reason was readily learned with questioning. She had become pregnant and her husband had insisted on an abortion, since they had two children. She had consented very reluctantly and felt very guilty afterwards. Now she was "hanging her head in shame," she remarked. Thus there was organ language operating, and also self-punishment over having done something for which she felt so guilty. Torticolis is often very painful because of the tightness of the muscles involved.

The seventh of our keys is *past experiences.* At least one incident in the past is usually located as one of the causes of most illnesses which are psychologically caused. Imprints arise from some past experience. Masochism stems from guilt feelings, usually resulting from past experiences. Conflicts can develop from past incidents.

Another type of past experience is that which is traumatic – very frightening or very threatening. Death of a member of the family may be a great trauma. You may remember a motion picture of a few years ago called "Three Faces of Eve." It was about an actual case, a young woman who had developed three different personalities, a splitting of personality. Among other causative factors was a very traumatic experience as a young child when she had been forced by her parents to kiss the face of her dead grandmother. The shock brought the split in her personality.

One possible cause of stuttering can be some very frightening event. In three different cases of young men with this speech difficulty such a trauma was located. All had been sexually molested in childhood by an older boy or an adult, following which the boys had been told they would be killed if they ever told. In addition to the actual trauma, there was thus an imprint set up. Taking this literally by the subconscious, the fixed idea was imprinted that they would die if they told, and "told" did not mean literally only of this experience but meant "talked." Then, with the need to speak encountering the imprint not to speak, stuttering resulted. With our questioning method all of these seven possible causative factors can be explored, no matter what symptom, illness, or condition is present. It should be made sure that all which have an effect have been brought out. Those of no importance are disregarded.

Insight, an understanding of the causes of the condition, may be enough to bring it to an end. On the other hand, there must be a digestion of this insight, a change of viewpoint on the part of the subconscious. This may be immediate or may require a little time. The difficulty is not in the conscious mind, but is in the subconscious. The inner mind must be led to understand that the uncovered causes need not continue to have an effect. Hypnotic suggestion can help to accomplish this. Further questioning can show if the condition had been eliminated. If not, further work may be necessary to gain acceptance from the inner mind.

The therapist sometimes will locate all the causes quickly and readily, without encountering resistances. Sometimes a condition can be cleared up in one or two sessions. Much more likely several are necessary and not infrequently many are needed. However, these methods are far shorter than more orthodox ones in psychotherapy and, compared to orthodox psychoanalysis, more can be accomplished sometimes in a few sessions than in three or four hundred analytic sessions.

The time needed for self-treatment, when it is successful, will usually be longer than when a therapist is consulted. It should be realized that self-treatment may not succeed.

A rather interesting and unusual case was that of Mrs. T. She was referred to me by a physician in another city, the city where she lived. She phoned long distance for a Saturday appointment and informed me that she suffered from migraine headaches. When Mrs. T. came Saturday morning she surprised me by saying she was returning home that evening. Obviously she expected hypnotherapy to be a magic wand which would be waved and she would then be relieved of her headaches.

Mrs. T. said she had had an occasional migraine attack for many years (she was fifty-two years old) but now they were occurring at least once in two weeks and sometimes oftener. They were far worse in intensity and they were interfering greatly with her work. She was a school teacher. When I asked about her environmental situation she told me of a wonderful man she had married, but who unfortunately had suffered a stroke two years ago and now was unable to work, although he was not entirely incapacitated. I noted that she really eulogized the husband. Mrs. T. seemed to be a very positive character. She did not enjoy teaching but was now compelled to support the family, which consisted only of her husband and herself. They had one married daughter aged twenty-nine but unable to help financially.

Obtaining her history took almost a half hour, and more time was required to explain the answering of questions by means of the pendulum. The seven common factors which could be involved were explained to her, with frequent interruptions on her part. A tape recording was made of the entire session and here is the way questioning was carried on.

Q.   Are you identifying with someone else close to you who suffered from this type of headache?

A.   No. (Pendulum)

Q.   Is your environment such that you are having your headaches because something "is a headache to you?"

A.   No.

Q.   Is there some motivation for the headaches? Are they serving some purpose?

A.   Yes.

Q.   Could the purpose be to get you sympathy and attention?

A.   "That's rather ridiculous. I'm not that childish!" This was verbal of course and the pendulum confirmed this with the negative reply.

Q.   Is there an imprint, or more than one imprint, which is causing you to have these headaches?

A.   No.

Q.   Are you tending to punish yourself by having the headaches, for they certainly are painful and most unpleasant.

A.   Yes.

Mrs. T. "Well, that's certainly not the right answer. I can tell you I'm not punishing myself. That's quite ridiculous!

Q.   Perhaps not, but often people will unconsciously punish themselves and not be aware of doing so. Your inner mind seems to think you are punishing yourself with the headaches.

A.   Yes. (Pendulum again).

Mrs. T. "Hmph. I don't believe it."

Q.   Is there any conflict in your mind that could serve to bring on the headaches?

A.   Yes.

Mrs. T. "Conflict? I don't know of any conflict. You say a conflict is wanting to do or have something and not being able to, being prevented. Well possibly I have some conflict over my teaching. I certainly would rather not have to teach or work at all!"

Q.   Is the conflict over your work?

A.   Yes.

Q.   Is there any other source of conflict?

A.   Yes.

Q.   Is there any other past experience which has to do with your headaches, one not connected to conflict or motive or self-punishment?

A.   No.

Q.   We seem to have three factors acting to cause the headaches. We'll try to find out more about them, but there may be something else involved. Everyone at times is frustrated, becomes angry, has feelings of hostility. These are normal emotions, but sometimes children are taught that they are bad emotions, which must never be felt or shown. Bottling them up is often one cause of migraine. Let's find out if you are bottling up some of these emotions. Is that the case?

Mrs. T. Of course not. I never allow myself to get angry. Sometimes I get a little frustrated but I'm never really angry.

Q.   Let's see what the pendulum says about it. Do you tend to bottle up such emotions.

A.   Yes.

Q.   Do you feel it wrong to have them — that it's wicked to
        feel angry and hostile?

A.   Yes.

Mrs. T. Well, maybe I do bottle them up.

Mrs. T. was then hypnotized and it was evident that
she was resisting, although she reached a light stage of
hypnosis. In hypnosis it was brought out that she had great
conflict over her environmental situation. She resented the
fact that she must work because her husband was unable to
do so. Her feelings toward him were mixed. She respected
him but was full of resentment at the situation and she was
now directing this at him, unconsciously blaming him.

One motivation for the headaches was that they
prevented her at times from working, and the same time were
serving as a means of punishment for her anger and hostility.
She regarded these emotions as definitely bad. A nice person
did not have such emotions. She was a perfectionist, as is
almost invariably true in migraine cases, and tended to punish
herself for not always performing perfectly.

At the end of her session, which had run two hours,
while she was still in hypnosis it was suggested that she could
now understand why she suffered these headaches and that
her subconscious could now end them as she had enough
burden with the family situation and did not deserve further
punishment.

I wrote the physician who had sent her to me, saying
that I doubted if I had helped Mrs. T. in such a short time
and that it would probably involve more sessions with her to
be sure of results. Some four months later he replied. He said
that Mrs. T. had returned home very indignant at me. I had
overcharged her, had done her no good at all, had not even

been able to hypnotize her. Then the physician added: "Strangely, Mrs. T. has not had a single headache since she saw you."

This was hardly a typical case either as to the time involved or as to the patient's attitude. However, it is an interesting one in many ways and the questions show how the pendulum is used to obtain information as to the reasons for her condition. Knowing that I would not see her again, I proceeded much faster than would have otherwise been the case. Self-punishment can seldom be dealt with and terminated so quickly. I suspect that her inner mind came to the conclusion that the need for self-punishment could be satisfied by the continued environmental situation.

14
Overcoming Character Liabilities

Character disturbances have wide variations, the worst forms being found in the psychoses (insanities). While not as serious, some of the neuroses also would be classified as character disturbances. Of course these require professional treatment and are not our concern here.

It would be a most remarkable individual who had no characteristics at all which could be detrimental and a liability to him. We might term good, helpful characteristics as assets and harmful ones as liabilities. Certainly no one wants to change or lose good characteristics, so it is the bad ones which are to be considered here.

It is very difficult to know whether Bill's bad temper is inherited from his bad-tempered father or whether it is merely a matter of identification, a subconscious attempt to be like his father. Identifications begin in childhood but may be maintained throughout one's life unless something is done to change them. It is quite doubtful if genes could carry such a characteristic as bad temper in Bill's hypothetical case, but it is a possibility. We have so many various characteristics in our makeup that a poor little gene certainly must be loaded, if all these characteristics are hereditary. Yet the genes do carry physical characteristics. It would seem that any inherited one would be more difficult to eliminate than one that is merely acquired, in which case habit enters the picture.

In trying to cause changes or to eliminate unwanted characteristics it is possible that the subconscious mind would know if one is inherited or acquired. The questioning technique offers a way to find out.

Most of us have a tendency greatly to exaggerate our liabilities and to minimize our assets. We may also feel guilty about bad characteristics, with a resulting need for self-punishment for having them. This would apply whether or not they are hereditary. In order to be rid of liabilities, the first step is to gain a proper perspective about ourselves, to see ourselves in the proper light. Many people look at themselves through the wrong end of the telescope. Having the proper body image is an important step.

Probably the most common characteristic liability is the well-known inferiority complex. There are few people who do not have some feelings of inferiority, at least along certain lines. For many of us some of these feelings may be of no importance at all. For instance if one lacks musical talent or ability — so what? He doesn't have to become a musician.

Along with feelings of inferiority there are usually other liabilities. Lack of confidence in oneself is one. An unconscious need to be approved is another. A poverty complex may accompany them. Almost everyone who feels greatly inferior is a negative thinker, and being able to think in a positive way is most important to success in this life.

Disregarding the possibility of a feeling of inferiority being hereditary, what would be its cause, its reason for being present? Probably every characteristic we own that is not hereditary comes from our childhood conditioning. Not many parents are experts in regard to child raising, and most make mistakes. If a child is not loved and given appreciation for his accomplishments as he matures, inferiority feelings certainly will develop. Confidence in oneself must be learned through experience. Lack of confidence brings fears of failure. And you cannot fail if you do not try, so some people become apathetic and make no more effort than is necessary.

If guilt feelings develop over weaknesses, then the situation is even worse, at least if guilt calls for self-punishment. Somewhat the same in effect are feelings of unworthiness, that you do not deserve something.

Essentially negative thinking is "I can't" while positive thinking is "I can." Accompanying negative thinking is negative behavior, and the opposite is true with positive thinking. Well-adjusted people who accomplish things are invariably able to think positively. It is even probable that the positive person will enjoy better health. He will have goals for which he strives, while the negative approach is to avoid goals as undoubtedly unattainable, so what's the use?

Several books have been written entirely devoted to the value of positive thinking and how to be rid of the bogey of negativism. They may approach it from different viewpoints, such as the religious one with prayer as a technique. There can be a metaphysical approach, or a matter-of-fact, common sense one. All are important and all are effective. It should be noted that positive thinking is very important in correcting other character handicaps.

Worry is another most unpleasant and restricting trait to possess. It goes hand in hand with negativism. Everyone worries a bit at times when things go wrong and then it would be a normal emotion, an example being when a person one loves is very ill. The chronic worrier, the "worry wart," worries no matter how well things are going. He will quickly find some other reason to worry if a current worrying factor is ended. Sometimes worrying is masochistic and the person actually enjoys worrying.

Perhaps chronic tension should not be considered as a character trait but it is close to being one. Tension comes from stress of one kind or another, perhaps arising from some of the bad traits which we have been considering.

In working to correct and eliminate some of these detrimental traits self-hypnosis can be of value in several ways. It helps one to relax and to carry the relaxation over into every-day life. Relaxation relieves or modifies tension, although it does not correct the stress factors causing tension.

Essentially the "treatment" or overcoming of adverse traits is the same for all. The first step should be to find out something about a particular trait, which can be accomplished by means of the questioning technique. Is it hereditary? If the answer is yes, it may take a bit more effort to remove it, but it certainly can be eliminated nevertheless. If not hereditary, is it a matter of identification with a parent or someone close to you? This is frequently the case. Breaking of identifications is mainly a matter of recognizing them as such and using self-suggestion to the effect that you are going to be yourself and will no longer imitate the person being identified with.

Many traits are a matter of childhood conditioning and repeated urging by the parents. Perfectionism falls in this category, as do other traits. Habit is then involved. How can any habit be broken? An effort is necessary, rather than to let matters drift. Sometimes the best way to break up a habit pattern is to exaggerate it. This is true as to worry. If the worrier will make it a point to recognize whenever he starts to worry and then to carry it to an extreme, the pattern may well become so ridiculous that it is broken. The worrier then thinks to himself, "I really am not worrying enough about this situation. How terrible it is. It undoubtedly will get worse. It may affect my whole life. I should think of nothing else today, I must spend all my time worrying about this. I suppose nothing will do any good and I must accept it, but that's no reason to stop worrying. I simply mustn't think of anything else."

Applying such an exaggeration it soon becomes almost a matter for laughter. Repeated again and again over any cause for worry will tend to break the habit.

Another of our seven possible causes is *imprints*. Many character traits have developed because of some fixed idea which has been set up in the subconscious part of the mind. Again the questioning technique can quickly determine if this is true and one or more imprints is active. If the answer is yes, determine how many must be sought, perhaps only one. Find out details about it. When was it established — at what age? Who planted this idea? Where were you, in what location when it was set up? What is the exact wording? It may be helpful with self-hypnosis to regress yourself to the event where it was established and by running through the experience remove its effects. Your insight and knowing the cause help to do this.

Another possible factor of some traits is *motivation* What purpose can it be serving? The purpose may be something easily determined, or may be rather complex. Are you seeking something through this trait — seeking affection and approval perhaps.

The possibility of self-punishment because of some traits should be investigated. Questioning can give insight into such a possibility. Sometimes self-punishment is needed because of feeling some emotions. The most common ones are anger and rage and hostility. Some people have been led to believe by their parents that these emotions are bad and should never be felt. Of course this is not true. Having such an emotion is entirely normal. What could be bad about it is not the emotion itself but what behavior may follow the emotion. Anger might well be justified, but it might be quite wrong to hit someone in anger. It might be particularly unwise if the person is bigger than you! Regarding such emotions as "bad" is often true with migraine sufferers, as has been pointed out.

Insight and understanding of the reasons why an adverse character trait has developed is one of the most important factors in eliminating it. Of course the person must also recognize that such a handicapping trait is present, rather than overlook it. The questioning technique can be of great value in locating causes and giving insight.

As an aid to locating and then working to modify or eliminate such traits, here is a list of possible "liabilities." Undoubtedly still others would fall into this category. Negativism, worry, selfishness, egoism, sadism, depression, inferiority and unworthiness, anxiety, aggressiveness, passivity, irritableness, laziness, indifference, masochism, perfectionism, impatience, inefficiency, indecisiveness, procrastination, etc. These are not listed in any particular order of importance. Some, of course, are far more detrimental and handicapping than others, but all are to be classed as liabilities.

If a person possesses many of these traits he is certain to be disliked by others, hence faces a great handicap in being successful. He may even be thoroughly disliked.

Usually adverse traits such as those mentioned develop from childhood conditioning, though heredity may be involved with some. There may be unconscious needs involved. It is well known that a bully usually is covering up his inner feelings of cowardice, compensating for it. A need to be loved may cause a person to be subservient to others, to do almost anything which might serve to bring attention and love. Recognition of the possibility of such needs and questioning about them can help in being rid of them.

15
Ending the Cigarette Habit
with Self-Hypnosis

Currently a strong campaign is being waged to induce people to stop smoking cigarettes. The main reason advocated for quitting is health. Lung cancer and other respiratory diseases are caused by smoking. There is no doubt of this being a fact. Unfortunately the tendency is for the individual smoker to believe that "someone else may develop cancer but it will not happen to me."

There are many other perfectly good reasons aside from health which should act to cause people to give up the cigarette habit, but it seems to be very difficult for most people to quit. Some six million dollars a day accrues to the U.S. government from cigarette taxes. to say nothing of that paid to the state governments. If our legislators wanted to take action that would lead millions to quit, and best of all would prevent juveniles from beginning to smoke, it could readily do so. How many people would smoke if each cigarette cost a dollar? Not very many. The youngsters would be unable to afford cigarettes. If taxes were increased so that a pack of cigarettes cost a dollar many people would be forced to stop smoking because of the expense. The remedy is quite obvious but oh, that nice tax money!

In preparing to write a book on how to stop smoking with self-hypnosis a lengthy study of the problem was made. I consulted scores of people who had quit, and more who had tried to stop but found that they could not do so. It has been said that cigarette smoking does not cause addiction but that is not true. Many are addicted and it is far more than a noxious habit which has been formed. From my inquiries, however, one fact became apparent. Many people, including definite addicts had been able to stop smoking with almost no trouble. It was said to me frequently, "Oh, I just decided to stop and I really wanted to, so it was easy."

That sentence tells the story. Almost anyone who really wants to stop smoking can do so and most will have very little difficulty, this including those who have smoked as many as three packs a day. The secret is in wanting to stop. Those who have trouble think they should stop, but really don't want to do so.

There is no doubt that hypnosis can be of great help to the person trying to stop. Many people have come to me for help with this problem. Almost every-one has tried to stop and has failed. Most are addicts and most have smoked at least two packs a day. I can give some fairly accurate statistics as to results with the method I advocate. Two out of five are able to stop with very little trouble, half of them saying it was almost like a magic wand had been waved and all desire had left. They hardly ever gave smoking a thought, even the first day after quitting. Another 40 percent were able to quit but had difficulty, some of them great difficulty. Ten percent were failures and did not stop. It should be added that this 10 percent included those where smoking is a psychiatric problem, with self-destruction a part of the picture.

The best effects where hypnosis is used in this connection is for the person who wishes to quit smoking to have professional help. However if self-hypnosis is learned, it can be effective. The method I advocate will be given here briefly.

The first step in quitting is to write out every motive you can think of as to why you should quit. The most important is health. Another one is cost. Two packs a day will cost about seventy cents. The cost in a year is over $260. If the person continues to smoke for thirty years it will cost over $7800. That's a tidy sum and it is only one part of the expense. Matches will amount up in the long run. Then there is the expense for burns on furniture and clothing.

There are many other motives for quitting, including serving as a good example for the benefit of your children, a most important reason; to be free of coughing and bad breath; to have more energy; to relax better; for cleanliness; and for proving to yourself that you can quit — accomplishment.

As to the rest of your program, set up a day for quitting at least three days ahead. Now change your brand of cigarettes, a strong one instead of a mild one, or vice versa; a type without filter if you have been smoking filter tips. On the day before you quit smoke approximately double the quantity you usually smoke. I might say that by that night you certainly will be fed up with smoking and anxious to quit!

Obtain from any drugstore some of the drug lobeline sulphate which is sold under various brand names. It is supposed in advertising to eliminate desire and to make quitting easy. Those who have tried it deny that it is very effective, but is does have some effect and probably acts to counteract the nicotine in your system. Take it for a few days. Also obtain from your physician a supply of a tranquilizer, enough for a week or ten days. Start taking the tranquilizer at once. It will help you to be relaxed and freer of tension.

Any drug store can also provide an imitation cigarette. Here anything will do as a substitute, a cigarette holder, a four inch wooden rod about one-fourth inch in diameter. This cigarette substitute can be held in your mouth at times when you may want to smoke. Another supply you may need is some chewing gum or some Lifesavers, something to pop into your mouth. During this preliminary period commit yourself to your friends. Let them know you are going to quit. Here you will meet with many negative suggestions which you will be offered helpfully. "Oh, you'll never quit!" "You don't really think you can quit, do you?" and other encouraging statements. Don't let them affect you. You *can* quit. When you've told everyone you intend to quit, it would be most embarrassing to fail.

Having learned self-hypnosis you will now use it and will give yourself suggestions which will help you. Suggest that you will have little or no difficulty in quitting: that the desire will be gone; that your subconscious mind is to help you in every possible way. Writing out your motives for quitting is intended to influence that part of your mind, just as your suggestions will. Add any suggestions which will stir up determination and particularly those which can make you really want to quit. State this to yourself while self-hypnotized — that you are tired of being addicted to a weed and that you want badly to be free of it.

When the day arrives for you to quit, take a positive attitude toward the matter. Of course you can quit. Of course it will be easy. How good it will be to be free of the habit. If thoughts of wanting to smoke do occur, you must immediately counteract them by thinking, "No, I'm through, I don't need to smoke, I don't want one." Each night for a few days when you go to bed mentally pat yourself on the back for having gone through that day without smoking and suggest that the next day will be even easier.

For the next few days after quitting, on arising in the morning, immediately put something into your stomach, such as a glass of orange juice. After breakfast brush your teeth using a strong mouthwash. Take your tranquilizer and lobeline sulphate. Read over every day for a time the motivations for quitting which you have written out. During the day, or that evening, use self-hypnosis, perhaps also during the day if it is convenient.

Each day is easier and most people find only the first three days very difficult. Even these days do not need to be tough ones. Carry this program on for about ten days and by that time you will seldom be thinking of smoking.

Many people find that they gain weight when they stop smoking. This is quite unnecessary if you are aware of the tendency. One reason for this is that your taste buds begin to function in a much better way. When foods taste better, you may want to eat more, but this tendency is readily controlled when you are aware of it. Suggestions while in self-hypnosis can also be helpful here. It might be well for a few days to watch your diet strictly, avoiding the carbohydrate foods which tend to cause fat, and sticking to the proteins.

Your mental attitude toward this program is very important. If you go at it skeptically and with negative thinking, you are going to find it hard to quit and may fail. With a positive viewpoint and determination to be successful, you will probably be surprised how the methods I have outlined will make it relatively easy for you to stop.

16
Hypnosis in Education

In the field of education unfortunately hypnosis has had little use and little scientific exploration as to its possibilities. Like the general public, educators have looked at hypnosis with lifted eyebrows and been afraid of it. In most colleges and universities few members of the psychology staff are familiar with hypnosis and most know nothing about it. In the psychology courses at most schools, hypnosis is seldom mentioned. School policy sometimes even forbids a demonstration of hypnosis in psychology classes. This attitude is changing as hypnosis is becoming more and more acceptable in professional practice, but it still persists.

I suspect that students, the younger generation, are much more open-minded and less fearful about hypnosis. In my practice where I have had students as patients I have yet to have one object to hypnosis or being hypnotized. This attitude certainly is reflected in the experimenting by students with marijuana and the psychedelic drugs. As a side comment, hypnotic age regression to a time when LSD was taken can reproduce the experiences under the drug – a cheaper and just as effective way of having psychedelic experiences. It is also safer!

Scientific reasearch into hypnosis and its uses is badly handicapped by lack of funds. Grants for such research are hard to obtain, even by universities and other institutions. Foundations which give funds for research are usually cold to hypnosis, although some funds have been granted. The U.S. Department of Public Health has made a number of grants, as have a few foundations.

An indication of the attitude encountered with requests for research can be well illustrated. A few years ago when the Ford Foundation was approached for funds, one of its consultants, the head of the psychology department of a large state university, in refusing funds states that there was no one of sufficient scientific standing and ability qualified to conduct research in hypnosis – an utterly astounding statement. Evidently he had no knowledge that many psychiatrists, other physicians, and psychologists have undertaken valuable research and have reported on it in scientific journals.

With many millions of dollars spent on research in medicine and other scientific fields, the amount available for any research as to the mind is negligible. Despite Freud's work, we know little about the mind, and even less about the inner part – the subconscious. Far, far more is spent on cancer research alone than is devoted to learning more about our mentality.

Nevertheless some hypnotic research is conducted, often at the personal expense of the individual engaged in some project. Stanford University has a Laboratory for

Hypnotic Research and has been able to secure funds. Work is being carried out at other schools and institutions and by individuals. Some has been of great value, some has been of little importance.

So that you will be informed as to what has been done in applying hypnosis to educational problems, some of the scientific reports which have been published should be discussed. The investigators whose names are cited are physicians, including psychiatrists, or psychologists or educators, all experienced with hypnosis.

White, Fox and Harris investigated hypnotic hypermnesia for recently learned material. There was no attempt in this work to give suggestions to promote recall, merely noting if recall was spontaneously better with subjects under hypnosis. First they were given meaningless material to memorize. There seemed to be no better memory for this than with a control group who learned the same material when not hypnotized. However, when meaningful material was used, the reasearchers found much better recall with the hypnotized group. Hypermnesia for meaningful material was definitely present. If suggestion had also been made, it is probable that memory would have been even better.

To comment, memory is a part of the subconscious mind. What motivation could there be for the subjects to remember something without meaning? Why should the subconscious bother to remember nonsense? It didn't! The subconscious works in a very practical way. What would be the use of recalling something of no value? Other studies of this nature by different researchers have confirmed the findings of this group.

William Fowler at Albany State College worked with twenty-five students, both graduates and undergraduates using hypnosis. The goals of his study were to increase retention and recall; to produce better concentration, and also better comprehension; to develop a love for reading and good scholarship; to increase the student's reading rate; and to develop confidence in the student's academic ability. You should note that most of these goals are those almost anyone would have in using hypnosis for study.

Fowler's results were excellent. There was 80 percent better memory, 94 percent better concentration, 66 percent better comprehension, 57 percent faster reading, 66 percent more confidence, 91 percent better scholarly approach to college work. Fowler's work was with students having difficulty in their studies, not the average student. Hypnotic suggestion caused the improvement. This research shows something of the possibilities for the reader.

Krippner at Kent State College taught a number of students self-hypnosis to improve reading ability, and reported good results.

He also worked with forty-nine elementary and secondary school children in a reading clinic, using hypnosis with nine of them, aiming at increasing motivation, decreasing tension. Even their spelling improved.

Another psychologist who has used hypnosis in promoting better ability to study and learn is Dr. R. L. Sprinkle at the University of Wyoming.

Getting at the University of Alberta attempted with self-hypnosis to better the ability of a group of students to concentrate. He felt that there would be better results if the word hypnosis was not mentioned. Indirect induction methods were used with the students thinking they were learning a way of relaxing, this being a disguised technique. The results were excellent.

Another interesting experiment with a single subject was by McCord and Sherrill in Denver. The subject was a mathematician. Under hypnosis he was given suggestions of being able to do calculus problems post-hypnotically with great accuracy and much faster than ever before. After being awakened, he did two hours work on calculus problems in only twenty minutes.

Erickson, a psychiatrist, claims to have worked with nearly one-hundred professional men, physicians, psychologists, attorneys, and others who had to take examinations and who exhibited what Erickson termed "examination panic." Many had failed previous exams and were certain they would fail again. Professionally it was a necessity for them to pass. Erickson used hypnosis and suggested that they would easily pass but only with bare passing grades. High grades were not important as it was necessary only to pass. Almost all his subjects were then successful. Most received much better than passing grades. Erickson felt that making only a passing grade instead of trying to do very well removed strain and anxiety which tended to block these people from doing well.

Most of the work with hypnosis in education has been by individuals clinically rather than as research. Many physicians and psychologists who use hypnosis have utilized it with students on an individual basis to help them in studying. Sometimes this was merely a matter of teaching them self-hypnosis so they could study better. In other cases it was to overcome blocks which prevented the student from doing well. Some cases of my own and others will be described later.

In my own particular experience I have worked with a number of students, some in high school, most of them in college, and sometimes with professional men such as were dealt with by Erickson. With every one their grades improved after learning self-hypnosis.

An interesting application here was told to me by a student at a California college. This was a young man who had been born blind. His mother and friends would read him his lessons and he did very well in school. He became interested in hypnosis when my book *Self-Hypnotism* was read to him. He found he was an excellent subject and learned self-hypnosis, having his lessons read to him while in hypnosis. He found this of such value in his own case that he began to hypnotize some of his college friends and teach them self-hypnosis. Some thirty of them learned this and invariably their grades improved. While hypnotizing friends is not to be recommended, he was of much aid to his friends. An aftermath to this was that the college authorities learned about it. Scandalized, he was prohibited from doing more with it with other students!

17
How to Use Hypnosis for Study

The methods given here are intended to help students who could be said to be "normal" in that no psychological or emotional factors are affecting their ability to study well. Of course students, like everyone else, vary considerably as their mental abilities and intelligence. One with a high IQ certainly finds it easier to study and will usually earn higher grades than others not so gifted. It might be thought that such a person would have little need of learning self-hypnosis, since he does so well without it. Undoubtedly it would offer less advantage to him, but the benefits are such that it will pay even the most brilliant student to learn it.

At the other extreme we have the person who is barely "getting by" with considerable effort, or who actually may be failing and will not be able to continue school. Of course such a student will receive the most benefit in these techniques. The benefits will also apply to a somewhat lesser extent to those students who are "average."

While we will be dealing largely with book learning, this is only one though an important part of being well-educated. A broad education covers other things, such as social contacts, getting along with other people, school activities such as sports, campus politics, drama, and many other activities — even good health and physical development through sports or physical education. The more time that is saved through better methods of study, the more leisure there will be for other important activities into which the student may wish to enter. One of the important benefits in our program is that less time can be spent in study when study time brings more knowledge at a faster rate.

How fast do you read? The rate will vary considerably with the type of reading. It will be slower for scientific subjects than for interesting fiction. It depends on other things too, such as the size of the print and the width of the columns. The very slow reader of necessity requires more time for study than one who reads at an average rate or better. It is undoubltedly true that there is better comprehension with faster reading. The slow reader is too intent on the words rather than the subject matter. Speed reading courses claim to be able to develop the rate to an astonishing degree. President Kennedy is reported to have read twenty-five hundred words a minute and some have reached even higher rates. No matter what your own speed is in reading, there will be benefits in time-saving if you read while under hypnosis.

Somewhat faster reading seems to develop spontaneously. Usually there is no great increase in speed. Probably it will be about ten percent faster. Self-suggestion while in hypnosis can add to this. It might be worded somewhat as follows, "As I study and read while in hypnosis

I will be reading faster because I am relaxed and concentrating better. I will be very alert, though staying relaxed. All tendency to lethargy will be gone while I am studying. My eye movements will be rapid as I read, movements of my arm and hand in turning pages will be quick. If I am making notes I will write rapidly and clearly and my subconscious mind will sort out the essential material from what I am studying so that my notes will be made to the best advantage. I will be fully alert mentally at all times while I study and read under hypnosis."

In reading the induction talk in Chapter Seven you will note that the suggestions promote relaxation and that listlessness and lethargy develop. Even drowsiness is suggested. Of course these feelings are not desirable while studying. The hypnotic subject, if asked to move, does so very slowly. If asked to raise his hand to his face, it may be several seconds or even longer before the hand even begins to move and it will lift slowly.

Suggestions can overcome this situation. One of the ways an experienced hypnotist can tell if a person is in hypnosis is by watching his behavior. This is shown by his slow movements, the complete lack of expression on the subject's face, a fixed stare and glassy appearance of the eyes.

Once when I was visiting a physician at his office, he asked if I could always tell if someone was hypnotized. I answered that I thought I could if I observed the person for a few moments. He said, "Well, here is my secretary. Is she in hypnosis?" I said I would decide after I had watched her for a few moments, which I did. Then I told him that I felt sure she was not hypnotized. Both the physician and the girl laughed and she said, "Oh, yes, I am. Dr. Jones has given me suggestions of being vivacious, quick in my movement, very alert and showing much expression on my face. I am in a very deep state." They had thus removed or counteracted all the signs which would indicate to me that she was hypnotized.

This is important in that when you have learned self-hypnosis you can make similar suggestions so that you can be alert, able to make normally rapid movements and lose any feeling of lethargy. This should be practiced, along with opening your eyes, before beginning your program of study. It will facilitate faster reading and hence more can be accomplished in the time devoted to study.

Anyone is more apt to concentrate better if he is interested in what he is reading, studying, or doing. Usually the student finds some courses more interesting than others. Elective ones tend to be more interesting than some of the required ones. Grades are usually better in the courses we like and find most interesting.

Poor concentration means less absorption and, of course, it is impossible to recall what is not absorbed. If your mind jumps around while you are trying to study; if you find yourself thinking about that blonde, the next football game, a party you plan to attend, you are not concentrating and are not absorbing, even when you pull your thoughts back to studying. They quickly flutter off again.

This is one of the most important benefits in studying under hypnosis — better concentration. There is some spontaneous effect here, but practice and suggestions will greatly improve the ability to concentrate. Wording of the suggestions could be as follows, "Whenever I study under hypnosis my whole attention will be on what I am studying. My thoughts will not wander off. Outside sounds will not disturb me and I will pay no attention to anything except the material I am studying. My inner mind will see that I am intent on this material, that I enjoy learning even if the subject is of less interest than others, for it is necessary for me to learn it. I will concentrate intently as I study. My subconscious will absorb this information, store it in memory. I will be able to recall it whenever it is necessary to do so. When I take an examination or quiz, or when I am called on to recite, I will be able to recall what I have studied."

An important research project was conducted by Dr. Peter Mutke at Monterey (California) Peninsula College on increased reading comprehension through hypnosis. Ninety-four students were used in the experimental group, and the same number were in a control group where hypnosis was not used. 85 percent of the first group were able to learn self-hypnosis. The Dan-Ro System of Remedial Reading was used in teaching the two groups. Reading speed and comprehension after five or six teaching sessions was about the same with the hypnotized group as that of the control group after twenty-two sessions. Results were from 200 percent to 1000 percent, with an average of 600 percent over the students' initial reading speed.

An interesting part of the test was the use of "image rehearsal" with the experimental group. Following each training session the hypnotized students reviewed the work, rehearsing it in imaginary situations in connection with reading, at school, in class, or during examinations. With this technique, actual reading practice outside the class was unnecessary. The greatest improvement noted was in the increase in recognition span tested by tachistoscope. Many of the experimental group reached the ultimate goal, compared to only a few of the control group of students. Dr. Mutke says, "These experiments . . . permit the conclusion that hypnosis is a most valuable tool in the teaching and learning processes."

The image rehearsal technique is one which you will apply in your program. While in hypnosis you can review the material you have been studying and use imaginary classroom and examination scenes, as though you were reciting or writing answers to exam questions. Depending on the kind of material you are studying you can probably think of other ways of using imagery for review.

Another technique for you to use is time distortion and subconscious mental review of the material studied. Dr. Cooper's development of the ability of the mind greatly to increase the speed of thinking can be of much value both in causing knowledge gained in study to be well absorbed, and also as a time-saver.

Time distortion can be induced at a conscious level, which probably would require a deep state of hypnosis. It can also be carried out at an unconscious level, this requiring only a light stage. If you become a very good subject and find you can enter a deep state, you can consciously use image rehearsal and can also consciously review the material you have studied, speeding up time and the thinking process. You can do this by suggesting that you are now going to take only ten minutes for this, but that it will seem that you are spending an hour for the imagery or for the review. Suggest that your thought processes will speed up to this extent while you are reviewing or forming the images.

If unable to reach a deep state, you can use the visual rehearsal at a normal rate of thinking, but can use time distortion for subconscious review of the material you have studied. When you have completed a study session, allow five minutes for your subconscious mind to review what you have just studied. This will give you far better absorption and hence much better subsequent recall.

For this, here are the suggestions you can use, while in hypnosis at the end of your study period. "I am going to relax now and my subconscious mind will review all that I have studied during this session. For the next five minutes after I say the word 'now' as a starting signal, my subconscious will review in detail everything that I have studied in this session. It will cover everything, just as I have studied the material, and will do this in just five minutes. It will store all this knowledge in memory and I will be able to recall it at any time whenever I wish to do so."

When you have given these suggestions, think the word *now* to yourself and then merely relax for the next five minutes. With practice you can perhaps cut the length of time for this subconscious review, taking only three minutes. Later you may be able to accomplish it in only one minute. As you are not aware of whether or not your inner mind is doing this, you may wonder as to success. Using the ideomotor questioning technique after you awaken yourself, you can ask if the material was reviewed. You might also ask questions as to whether your inner mind was able to do this completely in the allotted time of five minutes. Also you could ask if a longer time is needed; whether it can do it in three minutes, or in one minute. Use the information about this as obtained from your inner mind in later study sessions.

It is truly amazing and also ridiculous that in our educational system there is almost never any attempt made to teach students how to study efficiently, or how to take and prepare for examinations. Many who enter college drop out because they have never learned such methods and find they cannot fulfill college requirements. College authorities seem to take it for granted that their students have such knowledge, but those who have it have learned it themselves, without instruction. How to study and how to prepare and take examinations should be taught the student in his first year in high school, but I know of no high school offering such a course.

One of the points made in books as to how to study is that a regular program should be established. You should divide your study time as seems best, not allotting too much to one subject at the expense of another.

Another valuable technique which will be available when you have learned self-hypnosis is to listen to class lectures while in hypnosis. It should be pointed out that no one will be aware of what you are doing in such a situation or if you are in hypnosis while taking an exam. If you close your eyes for the self-induction, anyone who might observe you will merely think you are concentrating for a moment or two.

If hypnosis is utilized for class work, suggest to yourself that you will be very alert as you listen to the lecture and that you will absorb what you hear. If you take notes, suggest that your inner mind will help you sort out the material so your note-taking is thorough. You may find that your ability to develop hypnosis affects your results here. Trying this a time or two will allow you to know whether it is successful and valuable. Do not forget after any induction of self-hypnosis to awaken yourself at the end of the session.

A psychology professor at one of the eastern colleges wished to learn if hypnotized students listening to a lecture would have better memory for what was said than would an unhypnotized control group. About half the class was hypnotized with a group induction. The professor then lectured to the entire class. At the next class session he gave a test on the subject matter on which he had lectured. Grades of those who had been hypnotized were several points higher than those of the unhypnotized students.

In a written quiz or examination, when you have received the questions which you are to answer, you can immediately induce hypnosis. By this time in your practicing you should be able to do so with your key word or phrase with no more than a moment or two required. Read over the questions and suggest that the answers will come to you immediately for each one as you take it up. Suggest that you will write rapidly and that you will only use a proportionate amount of the time available for each question so that all will be covered. Suggest also that you will concentrate intently on your work and will pay no attention to possible distractions.

In Erickson's work with subjects, who were professional men taking examinations, a passing grade was all that was required. High grades had no importance. This is not true in school work, for you wish to receive high grades. However the main goal is to pass. Erickson's point was that when there is great tension and anxiety — what he termed "examination panic" — it is much easier to earn a high grade when the goal is merely to pass. This relieved tension and these subjects did well.

There is no doubt that some students achieve high grades in class work but fail miserably in exams due largely to their fears and anxiety and the tension that results. Some other factors can also act as blocks.

If you can take exams in your stride, you should aim for high grades. With the methods you are learning you should attain them with no difficulty. If you are having trouble with exams, then use Erickson's technique, suggesting to yourself that all you want is a passing grade and that this will come easily as a result of the studying you have done. Free of strain, you undoubtedly will do much better than mere passing.

All authorities agree that intensive cramming for an

exam is poor policy. It is far more important for a student to have a good, sufficient night's sleep before an exam than to sit up late cramming and then be worn out. If you have studied properly during a course, reviewing material at a subconscious level the night before the exam, while in hypnosis, is far better than cramming and takes little time.

Applying what you have now learned, the techniques given here, you should find yourself learning much faster, with less effort, and more thoroughly. As a result your grades undoubtedly will improve.

The application of hypnosis to education is a matter which has never been dealt with in any book and is important enough to have warranted much space here. Recently it was stated that forty million people in the United States are engaged in study of some kind, this from post-high school age on. It includes several million college and university students, also those attending business colleges and trade schools, older people in post-graduate studies, professional schools such as law, medical and dental schools, correspondence courses, adult classes in high schools, and every other type of school.

I once discussed the possibility of installing a voluntary program of teaching students self-hypnosis for study purposes with the dean and the head of the psychology department at one of the California state universities. They were interested and felt that such a program would be worthwhile, but finally decided against it on the basis that many college students are minors and there might be complaints and repercussions from parents for allowing their offspring to be hypnotized. It was a legitimate reason for not adopting the program.

18
Factors Which May Affect
the Ability to Learn

While anyone can profit and find study and learning much easier with the use of self-hypnosis, some people may have mental blocks which would make it more difficult. These blocks, unfortunately, are fairly common. When removed, the student's grades tend to be much better. Insight into these handicapping blocks is sometimes enough to remove them, and the questioning technique can locate them. They are unlikely to be known consciously, but are always known to the inner part of the mind.

Obviously a person of less intelligence does not learn as easily as does one with high IQ. Hypnosis is not a magic wand and certainly will not make anyone more intelligent. However, it can be of help in the use of such mental abilities as one possess, and in removing such factors as may block full use of these faculties.

Just how good a mind do you have? Many do not credit themselves with nearly as good a mentality as they actually do possess. The inferiority complex or feeling of unworthiness may be responsible for this wrong viewpoint. Past failures may lead a person to believe that he lacks ability when this is not true. Negative thinking is common, as has been noted, and it acts to bring unnecessary failure at times.

When these feelings and attitudes are present, they must be overcome through changes in viewpoint and a better understanding of yourself. Negative thinking must be corrected. Parents often favor one child over another, which can bring feelings of unworthiness. Rejection by parents is another factor serving to bring out this feeling. Some parents feel love for their children but are unable to display it and the child may feel unloved and inferior. Failures may make a child afraid to try for fear of failing again, with parental disapproval to follow. But it is through our failures that we learn and improve. Reviewing your childhood may help remove some of these negative feelings about yourself. Study can then be easier.

Identification with a parent or someone else who has been close to you may serve to keep you from studying well and getting better grades. Identification with a stupid parent, or one who may have handicapping blocks can affect the offspring. Sometimes a father may make remarks about himself which add to the identification factor. "I never was any good at mathematics." "I hated math because I was no good at it," and similar statements may take effect with the son or daughter.

Perhaps the most common factor acting to block one from doing well in his studies, or learning as easily as his mentality would permit is imprints. As has been mentioned an imprint is almost identical with a post-hypnotic suggestion and is much like a conditioned reflex, though it is not established through repetition. An imprint is rarely consciously recognized, but the subconscious will be seeing that it is carried out. It seems to be compelled to do this.

Imprints are of such importance that some examples will be cited. One amusing one, which had nothing to do with acting as a study block, was uncovered while I was working with a young woman. Under hypnosis, with ideomotor answers to questions, she brought out that she had been severely punished at the age of ten for some transgression. Regressed to this event, she said her mother was whipping her and scolding, saying to her, "Don't you ever say no again! Don't ever say that word no again!" On awakening the girl sat up and said, "So that's why I've been a pushover all my life. I never can say no!"

As an example of an imprint involved in learning and in study, a physician who himself used hypnosis sent his daughter to see me. She was nineteen years old and attending a California university as a freshman. She told me her IQ was supposed to be about 135 but that she was failing two courses and barely passing others. During her first two years in high school she had been an A student. The next year her grades slumped somwhat. And her senior year was worse. She complained now of being unable to concentrate. "I guess I'm just stupid." she remarked, sadly. "I must be a nitwit."

When an imprint is active, we often use the wording in our conversation. Her statement offered a clue. With finger answers to questions, she was asked if something was blocking her from studying well and was preventing her from doing well in her classes. The answer was affirmative. Imprints were then explained to her. Other questions and answers with finger movements were as follows:

Q.   Is there some imprint, or perhaps more than one, acting to cause you to get poor grades or to fail?

A.   Yes (finger movement).

Q.   Is there more than one of these imprints?

A.   Yes.

Q.   Lets find out about them. Let's consider the one which was first established in your subconscious mind. We want to find its origin. Was it set up before you were ten years old?

A.   No.

Q.   Was it before you were fifteen?

A.   No.

Q.   Was it before eighteen?

A.   Yes.

Q.   Was it when you were sixteen?

A.   Yes.

Q.   Have you been carrying out this idea since then?

A.   Yes.

Q   Was this something said to you?

A.   Yes.

Q.   Was it something said by a man?

A.   Yes.

Q.   Was it said by a teacher?

A.   No.

Q.   By a relative?

A.   Yes.

Q.   Was it your father?

A.   Yes.

Q.   Where did this take place? Was it at your home?

A.   Yes.

Q.   Was anyone else present at the time?

A.   No.

Further questioning brought out that it occurred in the home living room. She was then regressed to this experience. She saw her father, who was scolding her and was quite angry. She had made some foolish mistake in doing something she had been told to do. She felt humiliated and upset. "You're just stupid," her father had said, "You're a nitwit!"

Investigating further, she told of her father's characteristics. She was very fond of him but he was quite stern, a very impatient, irritable man, brilliant, and he demanded much more from her at age sixteen than she could accomplish. She brought out other incidents similar to the first. Repeatedly he had "bawled her out" as "lame-brained" a "dumb-bell," and other similar comments had been made. His scolding upset her and provoked varied emotions, including fear of his reproaches. Gradually she unconsciously accepted the ideas he was imprinting on her mind. Then her subconscious began to carry them out, causing her to appear stupid when she actually had an excellent mind. One way of accomplishing this display of apparent stupidity was to prevent her from concentrating well when she studied. Then she would get poor grades. Among other things, her father would scold her if she failed to get an A in any subject.

Understanding what was causing her difficulty made it easy to remove these imprints. Her father cooperated by letting her know that he really was quite proud of her, thought she was anything but stupid, and that it was only his irritability and impatience and interest in her that had led him to scold her. Within a short time her grades soared.

Another kind of imprint was affecting a twenty-four-year-old biochemist with whom I worked. He had earned a PhD from an English college at the ripe old age of twenty-two and was supposed to be mentally in the genius category. He held an excellent position doing research with an institution of great standing.

Don, as we will call him, told me he had had a remarkably easy time during his schooling. Study was very easy for him. He had what has been called a "photographic memory." He could read the page of a textbook once, then write out every word and every punctuation mark correctly. His grades were always at the top of his class. When he was twenty, something happened so he lost this rare mental ability. He had to spend many more hours in study, though still maintaining his very high grades. Now he had to work for them. "I'd like to know what caused this," he remarked. I might add that he was seeing me merely to learn self-hypnosis.

Ideomotor movements of his fingers, followed by age regression, located the experience that caused his memory to be affected. At twenty he had fallen in love, a rather typical case of puppy love, his first real love affair. After a few dates with the girl, he had asked her to become engaged until he completed his education. But, in a very emotional scene, the girl rejected him. Don was heart-broken and actually cried with his emotion. She was rather scornful in her rejection and told him, "Oh, go and forget it. Forget all about it. Just forget it and go away."

While this was not enough to be carried out completely literally, for he needed memory, it has served to affect it enough so that more impression was needed to remember things. His ability to read something once and remember it all was gone. When we had worked this out and he saw the cause of the trouble, his ability returned and his memory was then as good as before.

One of the most impressive cases of an imprint affecting mentality was one treated by a colleague of mine, a physician who is an instructor teaching hypnotic techniques with Hypnosis Symposiums. This occurred while we were giving a course in Honolulu. Among those taking the course was a physician who had attended medical school with our instructor, Dr. Raymond LaScola of Santa Monica, California.

Dr. LaScola made a tape recording of this case. His friend had a sixteen-year-old son who was in high school and was doing reasonably well but had never learned how to read well. He knew the words, could read them aloud or to himself, but seemed to have no comprehension at all of anything he read. It was necessary for his relatives to read his lessons to him and then he could absorb and remember.

In one session with the boy, Dr. LaScola located the trouble, using finger responses to questions. He immediately suspected some imprint as being involved. The answer to a question about this, brought affirmation. Something had happened at seven years old when he was in school. He had disliked the teacher immensely, for she had been very strict. With age regression he told what had occurred.

One day during recess another boy had thrown a ball and broken the classroom window. The teacher had blamed Harold, as we will call him. She would not listen to his denials and said he was lying to her. As punishment she kept him after school, handed him a book and told him he must spend a half-hour reading it and then must tell her what he had read. She then left the room. Harold tried to read the book and found it was much too advanced for him and was not a book for a second grade pupil. He did not know half the words in the book.

When the teacher returned she asked him what he had read. He tried to tell her his trouble and admitted that he had not read the book. She did not realize that it was too advanced, as she had not even looked at the book. In her exasperation she slapped him (provoking emotion) and said, "So you can't read! You'll never be able to learn to read so you'll understand it. It's beyond you."

Here was the imprint. It is rather surprising that this would completely block him as it had, but that was the result. He could read words and learn them but carried out the imprint and could not understand or comprehend them.

Dr LaScola gave Harold suggestions that, now that he could see what had caused his difficulty, this idea no longer need affect him. He mentioned that it was said to a child and Harold was no longer a child and now had an excellent vocabulary and could understand anything he read in the future. Some months later Harold's father wrote that the boy was reading perfectly and had no further comprehension trouble.

From these cases it will be seen that an imprint can cause trouble in learning. There may be none affecting you if you are having difficulty, but you can find out if any imprint is present with you by using the questioning technique. If you locate one, find out all you can about it with questions. Then regress yourself to the experience where it originated. Through insight you can probably remove it. Suggestions can also be made to your subconscious mind to the effect that, with understanding, it no longer needs to carry out the imprinted idea. Be sure to learn also if there are any other such imprints, eliminating all that may be present.

Questioning can also determine whether there are any other factors affecting your learning ability. Ask about identifications, and find the details if there is anything in this area affecting you. Find out if you are punishing yourself with failures or in other ways, and then try to locate the sources of the guilt feelings which call for self-punishment.

Everyone is the product of his childhood conditioning, and many past experiences affect us throughout our lives. Another question to ask of your subconscious is whether or not any kind of past experience is affecting your learning ability. Further questions can inform you of the details and, with age regression to any important event, you may be able to remove its effects. The removal of any of these psychological blocks and understanding of how they can affect you will certainly make school work much easier.

19
Hypnosis in Pregnancy

One of the most important applications of hypnosis is for childbirth. No doubt some readers will have no present interest in this subject and may prefer to skip over these chapters. Nevertheless, for the benefit of the females, especially those who may become mothers someday, this subject should be given detailed consideration.

If an obstetrician is available who uses hypnosis in his practice, it is of course the ideal situation for any prospective mother. Next best, if such a physician is not to be consulted, is one who advocates and practices so-called "natural childbirth" – the method offered by Dr. Grantly Dick Read in his book *Childbirth Without Fear*. Although Read denied it for some time, he later came to realize that his method tends to include the hypnotic trance. By carrying out the Read techniques, the pregnant woman frequently slipped spontaneously into hypnosis.

Most physicians who do hypnotic obstetrics follow much the same methods, which are similar to those of Read. On the patient's first visit, when it is determined that she is pregnant, the physician will discuss what should be used for her delivery and will suggest hypnosis, probably trying to dispel the usual misconceptions about it.

Incidentally, some obstetricians claim that the questioning technique is the surest way of learning if a woman is pregnant. If her subconscious mind gives a verdict that she is pregnant, it can be counted on and is better than any other test for pregnancy.

Early in the pregnancy hypnosis is induced and in subsequent sessions as deep a stage as possible is produced. The girl is also taught self-hypnosis so that she can use it during her pregnancy for better relaxation and freedom from tension, and also so that she can hypnotize herself on entering the hospital.

There are various applications of hypnosis which can be valuable during the period of pregnancy. There is a normal increase in weight at that time but this can easily be controlled by either the physician's suggestions, or with auto-suggestion and self-hypnosis.

As pregnancy progresses endocrine changes take place and the body is making various adjustments. Often nausea develops, the so-called "morning sickness." This may become a serious problem for the woman. Certainly it is a very unpleasant one. While there is a physical aspect to this, stemming from the physical adjustments and changes which are taking place, it also has an emotional side. This is further shown by the fact that women of primitive races seldom have much nausea. Excessive pain in childbirth is also a rarity with them.

This type of stomach upset is very largely a matter of

expectation and suggestion. When a woman tells her friends of her pregnancy a frequent question is, "Oh, have you had your morning sickness yet?" A most helpful remark! Also, relatives and friends may tell of the miserable time they had with nausea while pregnant.

Dr. Richard Clark of Los Angeles, who has been using hypnosis for years for childbirth says that he has invariably been able to end morning sickness by means of hypnotic suggestion. He is frequently asked by other obstetricians to visit one of their patients who has been hospitalized because of excessive nausea. Through hypnosis he has always been able to end their trouble at once.

Nausea is an unconscious attempt to eject something from the system, something unwanted or damaging. It may be merely an idea. If a pregnancy is unwanted, nausea may be an attempt on the part of the subconscious to end the pregnancy. Of course it fails. That may call for more nausea.

During a patient's pregnancy a wise physician will take the trouble to tell her exactly what to expect while pregnant and will go into detail as to just what she will experience during her delivery, and while recovering from it. At this time the questioning method should be used to learn whether or not any fears are present. Often fears may not be consciously recognized. If there are any, it is very important to dispel them. The common fears which may be entertained are of a very painful delivery, of giving birth to a defective infant, of having a stillbirth, or perhaps a fear of dying during the delivery. Another fear might be of suffering a miscarriage. These fears must be worked out and eliminated.

If self-hypnosis is being employed and the pregnant woman is not seeing a physician who is familiar with hypnosis, she should be sure the physician informs her fully of these matters. She can question herself as to fears, which may be found to be unconscious ones. If present they should be discussed with the physician, so he can correct them.

Delivery certainly will be much easier for any woman who has eliminated fears and has taken a positive attitude toward her delivery. Every effort should be made during the pregnancy period to gain these ends. It should be remembered that merely being in hypnosis and thus being extremely relaxed will raise the pain threshold and hence delivery would be easier for this fact alone.

Spontaneous miscarriage or abortion is not uncommon and sometimes is a serious problem for the obstetrician and the patient. Some women even seem to be abortion prone and unable to carry a child through to term. While there may well be physical causes for miscarriage, often there are psychological reasons which can be dealt with through psychotherapy. Hypnosis has been used most successfully in many such cases in overcoming this tendency, even after repeated miscarriages. Self-hypnosis could be of help but a woman with this problem certainly should seek professional treatment. Anxiety, fears, and tension can all play a part in causing miscarriage.

There are some other factors occurring in pregnancy which may also be controlled with hypnotic suggestion given either by the physician or while in self-hypnosis. Heartburn is one. This is usually described as a burning sensation in the lower part of the chest or the upper abdomen. It really has nothing to do with the heart and probably is a form of indigestion. Another possible reason is tension and inability to relax. A lengthy study of this condition has shown that most who suffer from it are very tense and do not know how to relax. Therefore the relaxation gained through hypnosis tends to modify or end this symptom. A physician can also advise proper diet and eating habits.

Another pregnancy condition which may develop is constipation, also related to the inability to relax. Hemorrhoids may develop along with the constipation. Regular bowel movements are important at any time, but more so during pregnancy. The physician's advice should be followed as to diet and use of laxatives.

Sometimes a pregnant woman develops a craving for certain foods, often driving her husband frantic with her demands. There is no real reason for anyone to crave odd foods but women hear of this being common during pregnancy and may expect it to occur with her. If such cravings are expected, they are apt to arise, but this is only a matter of suggestion and anticipation.

Some of the possible emotional causes for these cravings may be an unconscious desire for attention and to worry the husband, perhaps to annoy him by sending him out on errands during the night to find the craved for food.

Certain odors may become most obnoxious to a pregnant woman and her sense of smell may seem to have become more acute. Odors which have never been bothersome may become so bad and upsetting that nausea and vomiting results. There is no physical reason for such a tendency and again we must accept it as a psychological reaction. If this had never been heard of as a part of pregnancy, it undoubtedly would not develop. Probably it is only suggestion and expectation again at work.

Sometimes there is difficulty going to sleep at night — insomnia. All these matters mentioned here can usually be controlled by means of hypnotic suggestion and pregnancy can then take its normal course.

During pregnancy is also the time when the patient should learn to produce anesthesia. This can be through any technique which the physician may suggest. If self-hypnosis is used, the techniques which have been given previously may be applied. It probably is well to try both methods and discover which gives the best results. As a reminder they are by turning off the imaginary switches, or merely by using suggestion and developing glove anesthesia, anesthesia in one hand. This can then be transferred to any other part of the body. There are other ways of developing anesthesia. One which would be used by a hypnotist, would be to use an imaginary hypodermic needle and an imaginary anesthetic drug, pretending to give an injection in some designated area. The suggestion is then made that this will quickly bring on anesthesia.

A very effective, indirect method of eliminating the feeling of pain is possible. It can be suggested by the operator, or self-hypnosis can be used. It requires the subject to be in a deep enough stage of hypnosis to produce an hallucination. The operator, or you yourself, now suggests that you are going to leave your body sitting or lying in whatever actual position you are in, and that you are going over to another part of the room and observe your body. You can imagine that you are walking over and sitting down in a chair, then turning and looking at yourself. Now, if pain is stimulated in that body over there, you cannot feel it, because you are sitting over here!

Some obstetricians use this method whenever the patient has become a good enough subject to produce such an hallucination. After she is on the delivery table and the baby is about ready to be born, he instructs the patient as described above. She then becomes an observer and feels no pain as she watches that body on the table being delivered of the baby.

Dr. David Cheek of San Francisco, an obstetrician-gynecologist who is one of the Hypnosis Symposium instructors, does not feel that it is important for a woman to develop complete anesthesia during labor. He feels that merely being in hypnosis will raise the pain threshold so that pain is not too severe. Then if it can be raised further, the delivery will not be very painful at all. He develops at least partial anesthesia by asking the hypnotized girl to imagine that she is going to wade into a swimming pool, the water unheated and quite cold. First she walks down imagined steps until she is in up to her knees and feels the cold water developing numbness in her legs up to the knees. Then she is told to walk in further until the water covers her hips, and the numbness develops up to there. Then she walks in further until the water covers her waist. This produces either partial or sometimes complete anesthesia and she can then retain this after leaving the imaginary pool. When this has been rehearsed several times, she can do it while on the delivery table.

When hypnosis is to be used for childbirth, whether or not the physician is familiar with it, the patient should always realize that if for any reason she is having great pain, drug anesthesia can always be resorted to immediately on her request.

20
Childbirth with Hypnosis

Every physician who has learned to apply hypnosis in obstetrics has termed it the ideal method. Probably the leading exponent of hypnotic childbirth in this country is Dr. Ralph August of Muskegon Heights, Michigan. His book *Hypnosis in Obstetrics* (McGraw Hill) is the classic textbook in this field.

While many physicians in this country now use hypnosis in childbirth, the percentage of those who do so is still very small, not over 5 percent. Russia seems to be the country with the great use in obstetrics. There delivery is usually by midwives instead of physicians. In that country most midwives and many physicians have been taught hypnotic techniques in the medical schools, and it is the preferred method in obstetrics.

Dr. August has questioned all of his patients about their experiences with hypnotic childbirth. Every one has reported being pleased and has said she would prefer to have hypnosis again for any later pregnancy. Many of August's patients have previously had babies without hypnosis and thus were well able to compare results. Even those who had not been able to control pain found hypnosis of definite advantage. Other physicians have also reported that their patients always have expressed great satisfaction and the desire to have hypnosis again in any subsequent delivery.

What are the advantages found in the use of hypnosis for this purpose? The most important is not for the mother but for the child. It is the only method entirely free of danger to the baby. As has been mentioned previously, use of any drug also affects the baby and its respiration is depressed when it is born. The baby born while the mother is in hypnosis is not drugged and almost invariably takes its first breath spontaneously, without the necessity of any stimulus. Such babies are found to be more healthy, cry less, feed better, and are more contented.

For the mother the ability to have her baby with little or no pain is, of course, most desirable. Under hypnosis some women are able to shut off pain completely. Others feel pain but the threshold has been raised so it is not severe. With some, pain persists and drugs must be used. Even in this situation the anesthetist finds a much smaller amount of drug is necessary if the woman is in hypnosis. This is of value to both the mother and the baby.

Statistics show that the time in labor is reduced when hypnosis is used. This seems to be about 20 percent with a woman having her first baby. Those who have previously had a child usually are in labor a shorter time but this is further cut through hypnosis.

Another advantage is that there is less post-natal shock. The amount of bleeding can be controlled and the healing process greatly speeded up. Hospital stay (now very expensive) is shortened one to three days. There is an additional savings in expense if an anesthesiologist is not needed.

After the baby is born some mothers wish to nurse the child but lack enough milk. Others prefer bottle feeding for the child and want their milk to dry up. With hypnotic suggestion the flow of milk is easily regulated. It can be caused to flow more freely or to quickly dry up. Normally milk does not begin to flow until the third day after delivery. By hypnotic suggestion it can be caused to start flowing on the second day, or sometimes almost at once. This is an advantage for the baby.

About the only disadvantage in the use of hypnosis for childbirth is for the physician. It may require more of his time in order to teach his patient to become hypnotized. On the other hand, with delivery shortened in time, he may be at the hospital for a much shorter period. Most physicians make an extra charge if hypnosis is used unless women are taken in groups, when the extra time is not required. Teaching induction in groups is very successful. In this case a tape recording for the induction may be used, another savings in time for the doctor.

Are there contraindications for use of hypnosis in obstetrics? Very few, and they are identical for any use of hypnosis: it is not indicated if a person is extremely disturbed, very depressed, or pre-psychotic.

Childbirth involves effort and hard work. That's why it is called *labor*. If labor is prolonged, a woman will naturally tend to become very fatigued. Physiologically, fatigue is due to chemical changes in the tissues. These changes can largely be prevented by hypnotic suggestion, and thus fatigue in labor (or at any other time) can be greatly reduced or even completely inhibited.

Some of the old-time stage hypnotists used to demonstrate the inhibition of fatigue in a very spectacular way. Their performances were often given in one night stands in smaller cities or towns. Some stage hypnotists employed a trained subject who was taught self-hypnosis and how to prevent fatigue from developing. Often this was a young man who entered a show window, mounted a bicycle with its rear wheel jacked up. This would be twenty-four hours before the stage hypnotist's performance. The young man would then pedal rapidly for the entire period without stopping.

Sometimes a young woman would be employed. She would enter a show window similarly, but would sit at a piano playing steadily for twenty-four hours without stopping. In childbirth fatigue can be inhibited similarly.

Some physicians allow their patients to witness the delivery of someone else who is a good subject prior to their own delivery. This is valuable as it helps develop confidence in the patient who views this. She also sees just how matters will be handled by the physician and nurse. Some hospitals allow the husband to be present during delivery, if the physician concurs. You can find out about this in advance and have your husband present if you wish.

Here is the procedure you will follow for your delivery. When labor starts you will notify the office of your physician. Do not hypnotize yourself at this time. Do not try to develop anesthesia at this time. Remain calm and relaxed, have your hospital suitcase ready and prepare to leave for the hospital. You are not to hypnotize yourself until after entering the hospital, which helps prevent delivery until after you reach the hospital, for the baby might come sooner if you were in hypnosis and well relaxed.

The proper time for you to hypnotize yourself would depend on how good a subject you have become. If you have found you can only enter a light state, it would be best to wait until you have been taken to your own room and are lying in your bed.

If you have learned to reach a medium or deeper state your entry into the hospital should be the time to hypnotize yourself. As you enter, give yourself your signal such as the phrase "relax now" or whatever signal you have used in practicing induction. Use the counting backward and escalator for going deeper.

As soon as you have reached your room, develop anesthesia by means of whatever method you have found best. Prior to this you will have disrobed, been put into a hospital gown, and the pubic hair will have been shaved. You may be given an enema.

In your room you probably will be examined in order to determine the position of the baby's head and the amount your cervix has dilated. You will be asked as to the length of time between contractions.

You may keep your eyes open or closed during this time. It may be easier to stay deeply in hypnosis with them closed. Usually you can relax more during a uterine contraction with the eyes closed, and also you can concentrate better on your breathing. With the beginning of a contraction, take a deep breath. Then exhale and during the remainder of the contraction breath gently and normally in and out. Each time you exhale, concentrate on an imaginary spot in the center of your chest and listen to the noise and feel the sensation in your chest each time you exhale.

During this period you can give yourself suggestions for slipping still deeper into hypnosis and also suggestions for a greater degree of anesthesia, if you are feeling any pain with the contractions. A good suggestion would be, "If I feel the slightest hurt with my contractions the anesthesia will immediately increase until no hurt is felt."

You should also suggest that you will be aware but will pay attention to no sounds other than the voice of the physicians or nurses who talk to you. Some other woman might be in labor at this time who is not fortunate enough to have learned hypnosis and she may be crying and screaming. You can shut this out so it does not disturb you.

A nurse may question you from time to time. Unless she knows something about hypnosis she may be very curious and also she may not have been trained in the way to talk to a hypnotized patient. She may ask about your "pains" instead of your contractions. Knowing this, you will pay no attention to the word pain. You are having contractions, not pains. She may ask "doesn't it hurt?" or may say something else which is negative and which might cause you to lose confidence. Being aware of this possibility, nothing a nurse says will affect you adversely.

Physicians who use hypnosis for childbirth almost invariably teach the patient self-hypnosis. Procedure until the physician arrives at the hospital would be about the same whether or not your doctor uses hypnosis.

You may ask questions at any time of the nurse or physician. Feel free to tell about any unusual or different sensation you experience during your labor. You are completely aware at all times and those attending you should know this and treat you as they would any other patient.

After your cervix becomes fully dilated, the baby's

head will press down deep in your pelvis against the rectum and may give you the same sensation as you would have if you were about to have a bowel movement. You should tell the nurse or physician when you feel this sensation. Each time the uterus contracts it will be similar to your holding your fist real tight. The harder it contracts the more numb it will feel and you will remain relaxed. You can move about in bed and be in any position that is comfortable. If any medication or anesthetic agent is needed at any time for discomfort, you may have it immediately. It is always available for you.

At the proper time you'll be wheeled into the delivery room and will be transferred to the delivery table. Here your legs probably will be comfortably placed in stirrups or braces. Some hospitals have a mirror above the table on the ceiling so the entire delivery can be watched by the patient. If there is one, you could imagine it as a motion picture screen as though you were merely watching a motion picture of the delivery of a baby. Everything you see or hear will be interesting and nothing will disturb you.

If you've become a very good subject and have been able to "dissociate" yourself from your body, in the way that has been described, this is the time when you should do so. Imagine yourself somewhere else in the room, watching yourself on the table and watching all that is happening to "that girl" as if you were a spectator. You'll have no discomfort as you watch the girl on the table.

Throughout you will be able to cooperate easily and quickly with anything you are asked to do. You may ask any questions and make any comments whenever you feel like it.

As the baby's head presses against the bottom of the vagina and the baby's head starts to be visible, the tissue between the vagina and the rectum will bulge and look white instead of pink. If you are aware of this, give yourself a suggestion to go even deeper and that anesthesia will be complete. At about this time an episiotomy may be made, cutting the tissue so it will not tear. You will feel nothing but pressure if this is done. Suggest to yourself that the blood vessels will contract tightly in that area and will stay tight for a time. Thus you'll be able to control the flow of blood from the cut surfaces.

Of course if the physician is one who uses hypnosis, he will be suggesting these things to you all through your labor.

After the baby is born the physician will clamp and cut the cord. Soon the afterbirth will deliver. To help the uterus contract you may be given some injections in the arm veins or in the buttocks for the delivery of the baby and the afterbirth. When these are given, it will not bother you.

If an incision is made, it will be necessary to place several stitches in the tissues. You may be aware of touch and pressure but will stay insensitive to pain until it is completely healed.

You will then be taken to the post-partum floor where you will remain until you go home. When left there, remain in hypnosis and suggest to yourself that you'll quickly drift off into a good normal sleep for a time. Also suggest that your healing and recovery will be very rapid.

While in the hospital you'll be able to take frequent naps and relax completely using self-hypnosis whenever you may wish to do so. This will help your body to heal quickly and return to normal more rapidly.

The day you go home will be a thrilling one. After you arrive you should go to bed and relax. In the seclusion and comfort of your own home your daily routine of rest and baby care will come easily to you. You should take frequent naps or rest periods until your body has returned to normal. Restrict the number of your visitors and the length of their stay.

Probably the greatest value in the use of hypnosis for childbirth is the much greater relaxation obtained. If anesthesia can be induced that is also of great benefit. Many of the benefits are possible even if you are only able to reach a light stage of hypnosis. They are greatest if you have learned to obtain a really deep state.

Sometimes in practicing self-hypnosis, or if the doctor induces it, a person will only be lightly hypnotized but in the hospital will reach a much deeper state. Sometimes when anesthesia has only been partially obtained in practice sessions, it may become complete or nearly complete in the hospital. At that time the need and motivation is much greater, which probably accounts for this occurring.

Sometimes, though rarely, a very good subject during practice will become doubtful, frightened, and skeptical after entering the hospital and may only reach a light state or even fail to become hypnotized. If fears have been properly dispelled in advance, this probably would not happen.

It is always best if a girl goes through the training as it has been described here. However, Dr. August tells in his book of sometimes being asked to use hypnosis with the patient of some other physician after she is in the hospital. With strong motivation he has found such patients responding well, though never hypnotized before.

One of my patients was a young woman who had had two children, both very difficult deliveries. She had read about hypnosis in childbirth and on becoming pregnant again came to me for training in hypnosis, because her physician did not use it. She was an excellent subject and when the time came for her delivery was in labor only four hours, experienced no pain and left the hospital on the third day. Of course she was quite pleased with her results.

Two years later, Mrs. M. as we will call her, was again pregnant. She returned for a "brush up" on self-hypnosis. She was extremely confident after her previous experience. She remarked that it was all nonsense having to stay in the hospital for any time. She even wanted to be delivered in her home, but her obstetrician would not agree to that. She told me she was going home just as soon as the baby was born and the doctor had finished his work.

At eight o'clock one morning she phoned that her labor had begun and she was about to leave for the hospital. She said, "I'll have the baby as soon as I get there." At one in the afternoon she called again. "I'm home again," she announced. "It's a fine boy. He came just a half hour after I went to the hospital. I'm home feeling fine."

Of course this was a perfect case and most unusual. It showed, however, what her determination and confidence could do. Her subconscious mind evidently carried out all the firm beliefs she had developed as to what would take place. Her physician was amazed and at first protested against her going home so soon, but her condition was such that he did dismiss her.

A point that has not been mentioned is that if anesthesia can be induced under hypnosis, it can be reinduced or continued after the person is awake. A post-hypnotic suggestion can make this possible. When dental surgery has been performed the dentist may induce anesthesia and have it persist for several days. If you have become quite proficient with anesthesia you could cause it to continue for several days following delivery, but remember that a definite termination should be set. Several books are available written for the pregnant woman which describe in detail the entire process of reproduction. The more you know of just what will occur, the less fear there will be about it. Your physician can advise as to such a book.

21
A Recording for Childbirth

If your physician is not familiar with hypnosis and you will use self-hypnosis for your delivery a tape recording of suggestions will be of help to you. Remembering that repetition is one of the main factors in securing good response to suggestions, you should listen to the recording three or four times. This should be used after you have learned as well as possible how to hypnotize yourself.

If you are early in your pregnancy, learn self-induction as soon as possible. Then practice it only occasionally until about the seventh month of pregnancy. Then practice more often. During the eighth and ninth month use this recording. Here is the wording:

"You have now learned to induce hypnosis in yourself. Undoubtedly you've found it a pleasant experience. As you now listen, let yourself drift deeper. Take a deep breath and relax as you exhale. The ideas given you here are for your benefit so you can have your baby with the least discomfort. Your baby can be born without being affected by drugs and will be healthier, crying less and feeding better. Of course you want your baby to have these advantages.

"During labor you will be able to go deeper into hypnosis than ever before. You have a phrase to use and a formula which will let you produce hypnosis in yourself. When you enter the hospital you will follow your physician's instructions. You will immediately put yourself into hypnosis, or may do so after you have reached your room, whichever is most convenient.

"When you reach the delivery room your contractions will reach a peak and you will always be able to handle them easily and with courage. Labor is hard work but being relaxed makes it much easier. Opening your eyes will not cause you to awaken, but instead you will go deeper. Noises or voices will not disturb you and you will respond only to the voices of the nurses or physicians who talk to you.

"Every breath you take during your labor, and each contraction will be a signal for you to go deeper into hypnosis. Each contraction will cause the anesthesia to become greater. You will have no nausea, sickness, or pain during or after delivery. As the baby's head passes down the birth canal there will be sensations of pushing, stretching, expansion, drawing, pressure above the pubic area, trembling of your legs, but there need be no pain associated with any of these feelings.

"During your labor you can give yourself any suggestions which could be helpful to you so that you will be comfortable. You will remain relaxed, calm, numb and confident. Being aware you will be able to watch the birth of the baby and to take an active part. Seeing blood and secretions will not bother you, knowing this is a normal part of delivery.

"If an episiotomy is performed you will be able to control bleeding from the cut and to keep numbness and anesthesia in the area of your stitches until you are healed.

"After the baby is born you will feel only pleasantly tired and relaxed so you can sleep well at any time while in the hospital. During and after delivery you'll be happy, calm and courageous and able to take care of your baby when you are home and fully recovered. You will remember only pleasant things about your labor and delivery. You'll remember it as a most interesting, pleasant, rewarding experience.

"On returning to your room after delivery you'll drift at once into a deep normal sleep. When you awaken you'll be very refreshed, wide awake. You will heal very rapidly. All of the tissue, organs, and skin involved will heal quickly and your strength will be quickly recovered.

"Now you are fully prepared to have your baby at the proper time when it should arrive. You have learned self-hypnosis and know how to use it to the best advantage. You know just what to expect and the normal process of birth. You'll look forward to having your baby without fear or anxiety, knowing you will be properly cared for and glad you have learned a way to deliver it with the least discomfort.

"Your inner mind will carry out all the ideas and suggestions given you here. You will respond at all times to anything your physician or nurse asks of you or tells you to do.

"If you are going to breast feed your baby you can easily increase your milk supply if that is necessary. Milk ordinarily begins to flow on the third day after delivery but yours can start flowing copiously much sooner, as is needed, probably the next day.

"The morning after your delivery hypnotize yourself and tell yourself that your milk will soon begin to flow. In your mind's eye imagine each little milk gland increasing in size as if it were a balloon being blown up. See the glands as if they were a bunch of grapes, each grape quite small. See them all swelling up and becoming larger and larger. The milk is flowing into each gland. Think to yourself that you will now have all the milk needed by your baby. Repeat this process several times during the day.

"If you decide not to feed the baby but prefer bottle feeding, you will be able to dry up your breasts and prevent lactation. Suggest to yourself while in hypnosis that you want your milk to dry up as quickly as possible. Repeat these ideas to yourself several times during the day and the next day or two.

"Now if you would like to awaken, you may do so, feeling very relaxed and refreshed, feeling fine and coming wide awake."

22
Hypnosis in Dentistry

Most people, including dentists not familiar with hypnosis, believe that the main use of hypnosis in dentistry is the inducing of hypnotic anesthesia in the hypnotized patient. Actually this is only a minor use. It is too easy for the dentist to use novacaine or one of the newer anesthetic drugs. In most situations he will not resort to hypnosis for anesthesia.

An article in one of the dental journals once stated that 60 percent of the people in the United States had never visited a dentist. Only 40 percent ever go to the dentist. What is the reason for this avoidance of dentistry? To put it simply, it is fear of being hurt. This is in spite of the fact that modern dental methods are seldom excessively painful. It might be thought that another main reason to keep people from visiting the dentist is the cost. Every dentist has banking arrangements so that the expense can be spread out with monthly payments.

While hypnosis is now accepted as a legitimate procedure in dental practice, few dental schools have offered post-graduate courses in "hypnodontia." There are exceptions. The University of Oregon Dental School and the Kansas City Dental School have given several such courses, which have been well attended. Tufts, Creighton, the University of North Carolina, and still others have given courses. Hundreds, perhaps thousands of dentists have taken privately given courses such as those offered by Hypnosis Symposiums or other groups, including the workshops of the hypnotic societies.

The average dentist who uses hypnosis will probably resort to it only three or four times a week. A few dentists have become so interested and have had so many referrals for hypnosis by colleagues who do not use it, that they have become specialists in hypnodontia, applying it with all their patients.

No one looks forward to visiting a dentist. Even having your teeth cleaned, a prophylaxis, is not pleasant. The fearful patient is an excellent candidate for hypnosis. Even extensive dental treatment can be carried out while he is in hypnosis without it being much of an ordeal. A good subject can even have hallucinations induced so that he pays no attention to whatever the dentist is doing. He may listen to hallucinated music, or watch an hallucinated television program.

Most children are very fearful of a visit to the dentist. Pedodontists and other dentists who work with children find that applications of hypnosis with children almost revolutionizes their practice. Instead of having to work with frightened, possibly screaming, children, they play a game with the child, soon have him hypnotized and very probably sitting quietly in the dental chair, mouth open while the dentist works, but hallucinating an interesting TV program. An injection of an anesthetic drug will pass unnoticed. Children are such good subjects that they can develop a deep trance and almost any hypnotic phenomena can then be induced, including anesthesia if necessary.

Another situation where the dentist finds hypnosis of great value is with the spoiled brat, or the willful child who simply does not intend to submit to dental treatment. He wants no part of it and refuses to cooperate in any way. The dentist skilled in hypnosis knows how to handle this situation. In a very short time the child is in hypnosis and is being completely cooperative. He often will enjoy being taken to such a dentist for future work.

Hypnotic anesthesia does have its uses, although it is only one factor in the use of hypnosis in dentistry. Drug anesthesia wears off in a couple of hours. If dental surgery has been extensive, if there has been an extraction, there will be considerable pain when the drug has worn off. Here there can be almost routine application of hypnotic anesthesia. It can be induced by the dentist right on top of the drug anesthesia. It can persist overnight, even for several days if that is desirable. The dentist ordinarily will suggest some definite time for it to be terminated.

One dentist extracted a tooth from a woman patient who was an excellent hypnotic subject. In this case he had used only hypnotic anesthesia, no drug whatsoever. He gave her the suggestion that the anesthesia would persist and she would be perfectly comfortable, but it would end when she returned to his office five days later for a checkup of the work. Five days later she returned and on entering his office clapped her hand to her mouth and exclaimed in great pain.

Following the extraction she had had a dry socket, which is extremely painful. The anesthesia had persisted and she had had no pain until returning to the dentist's office. That removed the anesthesia! Of course the dentist quickly re-hypnotized her and reinstated the anesthesia.

Sometimes there are contraindications for the use of drug anesthesia, perhaps with a cardiac patient, and then hypnotic anesthesia may be resorted to by the dentist. If a patient is an excellent subject, the dentist may not wish to bother with drugs and will use only hypnotic anesthesia.

There are other dental uses of hypnosis. It is not uncommon for a dentist to have a patient who will gag badly whenever the dentist tries to work in his mouth. This is an awkward situation for both dentist and patient. No work can then be accomplished. With a patient in hypnosis, there is rarely any trouble with this situation. Suggestion will prevent the gagging and the dentist is able to work.

In a few cases suggestion will not end the gagging tendency. The patient continues to gag every time the dentist starts to work. It is then necessary for the dentist to take time and find the reason for the gagging. It can be located with the questioning technique. Invariably the patient is associating to some past experience where he gagged, choked, or vomited. The patient has no conscious knowledge of this. He merely reacts by gagging if anything is introduced into his mouth. In some cases there is more than one previous experience which must be located. The experience could be anything which had such a result, and almost invariably it will have occurred in childhood. Perhaps the most common experience is a tonsillectomy, where the child was not given a general anesthetic, or where he may have choked after coming out of the anesthetic.

Sometimes the past experience which promotes the gagging can be somewhat amusing, though it was not amusing to the child. When giving a class to a group of dentists several years ago, one of those attending was a "gagger." He needed extensive dental work himself, but could not have it done. At the attempt by another dentist to begin work, this dentist would gag violently. Using the questions and then regressing him to the experience to which he was associating, it was found that he had been taken on a fishing trip by his two older brothers, this at the age of five. After they had eaten a picnic lunch, a slightly older brother had wrestled with him, sat on him and then had taken a handful of angleworms from their bait can and pretended to put them in his smaller brother's mouth. Inadvertently he had actually dropped one in the brother's mouth, which caused him to vomit. When this event had been uncovered and worked out, the dentist no longer found it necessary to gag and he was able to have his dental work performed.

Another situation where hypnosis can be helpful is with bruxism, the tendency to grind one's teeth during the night. This can cause damage to the teeth, tending to loosen them, even grinding off some of the teeth. Malocclusion may be one reason for this but usually it has a psychological cause. This may be along the lines of organ language. "He ground his teeth in rage," is a common expression, and the bruxism patient may be doing just this, being filled with hostility, resentment and anger, which he expresses during the night in this way. Another possibility with a bruxism patient is that he is "gritting his teeth to bear it" — some environmental situation. Uncovering the causes with the questioning and thus gaining insight may overcome the tendency to grind the teeth. Hypnotic suggestion may also be of help here.

These are probably the main uses of hypnosis in dentistry. Of course just the relaxation that comes with being hypnotized is of value, for relaxation will raise the pain threshold to some extent. Pain is never felt as severely if one is relaxed instead of tense.

Even if able to use self-hypnosis it is probably better for most dental patients to have the dentist familiar with and able to use hypnosis. However, there may be no opportunity to visit a "hypnodontist." Self-hypnosis may be most helpful then. It should be explained to the dentist what you expect to do and that you want a very few moments in which to hypnotize yourself. In this situation you should be aware that the dentist is quite likely to offer some negative suggestions and statements, especially if you are able to induce anesthesia in yourself. He may be very skeptical and say, "Are you sure it is not hurting," or some similar phrase.

23
Some Other Uses of Hypnosis and Self-Hypnosis

When you have learned self-hypnosis there are various other applications aside from those which have been described. You may wish to use some of them. Some will depend on the depth of trance you are able to reach, and if you are able to develop hypnotic anesthesia. If you visit the dentist it is helpful to be in hypnosis for your dental work, even if you cannot induce anesthesia. The pain threshold will be raised through relaxation so you probably would hardly be aware of the needle if the dentist gives you an injection.

For minor surgery, as in dentistry, you may be able to anesthetize yourself even without reaching a very deep state. For major surgery a deep state would be needed if only hypnotic anesthesia were to be used, but this is rarely done. If you are in hypnosis when a drug anesthetic is used, a much smaller amount of the drug will be needed, which is a definite advantage. Some of the other applications in surgery can then be made, such as preventing shock, nausea, or retention of urine, and the speeding up of healing.

Being able to go deeply into hypnosis depends to some extent on motivation. Escape from pain, either in dentistry, for childbirth, or for any other reason, is a very strong motivation. This makes it easier to produce anesthesia. Dentists who use hypnosis find a much greater percentage of patients will produce anesthesia than when it is merely suggested as a demonstration of hypnotic phenomena.

Hypnotic anesthesia would only be used in major surgery if there was some contraindication for the use of drugs, as perhaps with a heart condition.

Modern living seems to promote nervous tension and many people have never learned to relax. Stress and tension can bring on many of the psychosomatic illnesses, particularly if these conditions are prolonged. Fatigue is also a by-product of these conditions. With hypnosis there is spontaneous relaxation which may be carried over after awakening. Of course nervousness and tension can build up again, but most people who have learned self-hypnosis find relaxation much easier. Of course you'll be much more relaxed if your problems can be resolved.

That tired feeling may be a result of physical exertion or it may be psychologically caused, as from tension. Worry and anxiety bring mental fatigue and lack of energy. People who are neurotic almost invariably complain of being fatigued. Fatigue can largely be inhibited through hypnotic suggestion, or even removed if it has developed. Physiological fatigue is a result of chemical changes in the tissues and muscles. The subconscious mind seems to be able to regulate this. Medically speaking not much is known about fatigue.

A psychiatrist friend once took me through a state mental hospital. There is a psychotic condition called catatonia, where the sufferer seems to have lost all contact with reality. He may remain perfectly motionless, cataleptic, even when in some very uncomfortable position, for hours, until attendants may force him to move. He may also suffer delusions. In an indoor court at the hospital I noticed such a case. A man was up in a tree, standing on one foot, with the other foot pressed against that calf. He thought he was a bird and every morning he was allowed to climb the tree and stay in this position until evening. He seemed to feel no fatigue in this uncomfortable position, and he never moved throughout the day. Fortunately, he made no attempt to fly!

Some hypnotic research has been conducted as to fatigue, with rather conflicting results. Some investigators have not been able to inhibit it in their subjects, perhaps because they did not use the proper methods. Some years ago a physician at Johns Hopkins Medical School had excellent results with a number of subjects. He would have them lift a two pound weight tied to a forefinger to the beat of a metronome set to beat once a second. After four or five minutes the finger would become so tired that the weight could no longer be lifted. Under hypnosis with strong suggestions of no fatigue, the subjects would continue to lift the weight for several hours.

Could inhibiting fatigue be dangerous? I presume it could if carried to some great extent, but this is unlikely. I think the teleology of the subconscious would again enter the picture. If inhibition of fatigue were to be damaging, I suspect that fatigue would develop.

To rid yourself of tiredness at the end of a day should be perfectly safe and quite desirable at times. Hypnotizing yourself for a few moments, with suggestions that you will relax and that all your fatigue will drain away can bring such results that you awaken very refreshed. It is best to combine visual imagery with these suggestions. Imagine yourself, in your mind's eye, engaging in some sport such as tennis, golf, swimming, or even merely walking around the block. See yourself as fresh as the proverbial daisy, full of vim and vigor. On awakening the tendency is to feel the way you saw yourself with the imagery.

Sleeping pills of one kind or another are sold by the billions in this country. This indicates how widespread are sleeping difficulties, people finding it difficult to sleep well, as nature intends. Unfortunately, the barbiturates usually prescribed for this condition may become addictive. They certainly are addictive in one sense because the sufferer from insomnia becomes dependent on the pills as a crutch.

It is very rare for a child to have trouble sleeping well, but even young adults often have insomnia. While no one ever dies from it, and most insomniacs are in very good health, it is a most unpleasant condition and can become a matter of serious concern to the victim.

Insomnia takes two forms. Usually the trouble is in going to sleep once in bed. The victim turns and tosses for some time, trying his best to get to sleep. Sometime later, perhaps after hours, he drops off. A factor entering here is that Law of Reversed Effect. Going to bed doubtful of being able to go to sleep, expecting to be wakeful, he tries to go to sleep and only becomes wider awake. Finally he stops trying and thinking about sleep and drops off.

With the other type of insomnia there is no difficulty in going to sleep but the victim awakens during the night or towards morning and then is unable to go back to sleep. He may get up and drink something, perhaps read for a time, and eventually sleep again, or he may remain awake until time to arise. A few unfortunates may develop both types of insomnia.

Overcoming this condition is sometimes relatively easy by means of self-hypnosis. Usually insomnia is merely a bad sleeping habit which has been developed, but sometimes it is a deep-seated neurotic condition. Then psychotherapy may be required in order to eliminate it. If it is merely habit, the sufferer can often find self-hypnosis a good way of getting to sleep easily.

To be successful, it is necessary to break up the old habit pattern. Instead of going to bed with the idea of lying awake for a time, it is best to take the attitude, "So what if I don't go to sleep at once? It really doesn't matter, for I'll be resting." The most important thing is not to try to go to sleep. And keep your thoughts off sleep. Try to think only of something pleasant.

Another factor here is that so many insomniacs take their problems to bed with them and think them over, worrying about them. Bed is not the place for problems. Your thoughts should be kept only on pleasant things.

In using self-hypnosis to overcome insomnia, hypnosis is induced on going to bed and on being ready to go to sleep. Then you should think to yourself, "Within a few moments (which is indefinite) I will drop off into a good normal sleep and will sleep deeply and well all night long." After repeating this suggestion three or four times, there should be no further thinking about sleep. It is important not to think about sleep as this will then prevent you from dropping off. Remain in hypnosis after having done this as the relaxation will help in bringing sleep. You can drift right from hypnosis into normal sleep.

Some people fall asleep best when they are tired, while others find that great fatigue seems to prevent them from going to sleep. For these people, being able to relax well with self-hypnosis and to rid themselves of fatigue will enable them to go to sleep more promptly.

When there are psychological causes behind insomnia and it is a neurotic symptom, self-help is more difficult as a means of overcoming the trouble. Insight into the causes is needed. Some may be very deep-seated and hard to eradicate. Self-punishment might be a factor, or identification with someone who suffered from insomnia. Possibly imprinting or other factors may be present. Sometimes the person unconsciously associates sleep with death, without realizing that this is untrue. We speak of death as the eternal sleep. With such a fear, the person fears to go to sleep – he might die. People who tend to have nightmares may be afraid to go to sleep because they might then have bad dreams during the night.

There can be still other reasons for having developed insomnia. The questioning technique affords a means of learning whatever is involved in your own particular case.

Being able to express yourself well publicly, and to communicate is a very valuable asset. Some people find it impossible to give any kind of public speech, even to a small audience. Some are too withdrawn so they even have difficulty communicating with friends or even with other members of the family. Reciting in a classroom may be very difficult and might result in poorer grades even when there is a good knowledge of the subject.

Perhaps self-consciousness makes it difficult to communicate. Ordinarily this is not hard to overcome. Gaining a proper viewpoint of yourself should correct this. When self-consciousness is present the difficulty in speaking may be only from a feeling of embarrassment rather than from actual stage fright. A bit of practice, such as joining a local Toastmasters' group is an excellent way of developing speaking confidence.

Real stage fright is more extreme. It may come from excessive self-consciousness and feelings of inferiority. Often it arises from some past experience, almost invariably one in childhood. This means conditioning. It would hardly be expected that an actor or actress would have such a difficulty except perhaps early in his or her career. However, some very prominent ones suffer from this and never get over it. Most lose their fright as soon as their performance begins. It is largely a matter of anticipation.

Before the late Marilyn Monroe achieved her success, she had several opportunities which she muffed completely. The moment she found herself before a camera or microphone she would freeze, in a panic, quite unable to move or to speak. Her physician sent her to me to see if this could be overcome with hypnosis. Marilyn proved to be a good subject. Various unpleasant childhood experiences were brought out which were related to her fright. When another opportunity came her way, she was able to handle it and went on to become famous, although she still had some qualms. Longer treatment probably would have made it still easier for her.

A reader who is handicapped in this way would do well to explore with the questioning technique and try to locate any experiences which could be the cause of the fright. It will frequently be located as some church or school entertainment or play where as a child you became frightened and perhaps forgot your lines or some little poem you were supposed to recite. Sometimes an imprint can be involved. Often these causes can be nullified and stage fright ended.

Stuttering is a most distressing condition in which hypnosis can be very helpful. Stangely, nine out of ten who stutter are males. For some reason most people who are so afflicted are excellent hypnotic subjects. One of the advantages in using hypnosis here is that most stutterers speak without difficulty while in hypnosis. When awakened, the speech difficulty has returned. However this shows the patient that he can be free of it. Self-hypnosis is helpful with the stutterer in teaching him to be more relaxed and in overcoming his feelings of inferiority, but self-treatment of this condition is not likely to be successful.

Problems as to sex are very common with both men and women. A good share of the work of psychotherapists is in treating sex complications. Frigidity in women, and impotence in men, including prematureness, are the most common and easiest sex difficulties to treat. Infertility, and homosexuality are still others, treatment being more difficult in these cases. In the latter case few homosexuals have any desire to change and nothing can be accomplished while this is true. The gynecologist encounters many menstrual difficulties with his women patients. It is impossible here to go into any detail as to the use of hypnosis in treating all these conditions but it often is of great advantage. Self-hypnosis is useful in some of these conditions but self-help is not likely to be very successful in many of them, though self-hypnosis may be useful.

While hypnosis may be of utmost value in the psychotherapeutic treatment of neuroses, these disturbances certainly are not likely to be benefitted by self-treatment, and it is contraindicated. There is one exception, and that is for some phobias. It is rather surprising how many people have a phobic reaction to some particular thing. Ordinarily such a person feels ashamed of his fear and it is known only to the members of the family or very close friends. There is a host of phobias which have received technical names, such as claustrophobia, the fear of being confined in a small space. Some are quite commonly held, such as the fear of high places.

If a person seems to be exceptionally fearful, has several phobias, it is probable that self-help would be of little value. Where there is only one, or perhaps two real phobias, self-hypnosis and self-treatment can often resolve the fear so it is ended, and the person is much more comfortable. In this type of case the fear in all probability is associated to some past experience of childhood, probably completely forgotten or repressed, or perhaps remembered but not connected to the phobia.

Popular magazines, particularly the women's magazines, frequently publish some kind of new dietary fad which will undoubtedly cause the reader to shed poundage rapidly if he follows it. Some physicians are obesity specialists and treat nothing else. Overweight is one of the biggest problems of our age, biggest in more ways than one.

Excess poundage is most likely to appear as we grow older and are physically less active. "Fair, fat, and forty" is one remark often made. If your weight is more than ten percent above the normal for your age and height, then it is technically termed obesity.

There can be many psychological and emotional causes for obesity, seldom consciously recognized. Any of our seven possible keys can be involved. Of course the problem is really not overweight, but overeating.

The usual medical treatment consists of offering a diet to be followed and prescribing a drug which is an appetite killer. If the overweight person continues on the diet and does shed poundage, a few months later he or she is right back where he started, having gained it all back again. Diet is a nasty word to the obese person. Few will continue to diet for very long. If only a few pounds are to be lost, this type of treatment may be successful, but even then the extra pounds are apt to accumulate again before long.

The real way to take off weight and *keep it off* is to learn the reasons for overweight and overeating and, with self-hypnosis make a change in your eating habits. Then there is much less likelihood of regaining the excess when you have lost it. Hypnosis is valuable for breaking former bad eating habits and in helping develop proper ones.

Without any need to go on a strict diet of any kind, it is advisable to change your pattern to eating protein foods and avoiding the carbohydrates. In doing this you eliminate the kinds of food which are fattening. While calories have importance, the kind of food eaten is much more important than the number of calories.

There are several approaches which will be helpful. Almost every obese person when questioned will admit that he bolts his food without chewing it very much, and eats hurriedly. Many are surprised at realizing this. Make it a habit to chew your food, to masticate it thoroughly and you will eat less. Make sure you are served small portions of food. The tendency is to eat everything on the plate, so be sure there's less on it. If you must snack, have foods available which have few calories and are not fattening. Several cocktails give you a good many extra unneeded calories. Keep your liquor intake to a minimum while reducing.

You'll probably find one of your causes for overeating is imprints set up in your childhood. Most children have periods where there is some eating problem. A parent, usually the mother, scolds and unknowingly establishes imprints which are then carried out. The wording of some common examples is, "You mustn't waste food," "You must eat everything on your plate or you can't have your dessert," "You must eat to be big and strong," and there are many others. Carried into adult life, as they are, you are bound to overeat compulsively.

There are several million alcoholics in this country. No really successful method of treatment has ever been devised for this condition. Undoubtedly the most successful has been the helpful counselling of other alcoholics in Alcoholics Anonymous. Medically speaking we do not know very much about the causes of this problem. Some physicians now believe that there is a physical factor present, something like an allergy. There certainly are psychological factors working.

Like stutterers, alcoholics often are excellent hypnotic subjects, though this varies with the individual. I have found hypnotherapy very helpful with alcoholics. There is failure with most cases, but there are also many real successes. Last Christmas for some reason I received a card from a former woman alcoholic patient. She managed to consume a fifth of whiskey every day when I first saw her. That had been fifteen years ago and she merely said on the card that she wanted me to know that she'd never had a drink since she had stopped seeing me. There have been a good many other successful conclusions to hypnotherapy with my patients, and with most there has been failure. Alcoholism is a very difficult problem to overcome.

Recently there have been magazine articles published exposing the frequent use of drugs in sports to increase athletic ability, mainly the amphetamines. The side affects may be detrimental. Not long ago one of the leading French bicycle riders died as a result of taking such a drug during a race. Many coaches and trainers in both professional sports and in the colleges resort to these drugs for their athletes.

It is quite surprising to professional men familiar with hypnosis that there has not been more use of hypnosis as a substitute for drugs. It is far better than drugs in effect. Professional athletes whose abilities are financially very rewarding are certainly overlooking something which could help them earn or even increase their rewards, and quite safely.

Some years ago one of the professional baseball teams hired a hypnotist to work with the members of the team. This project was bungled and mishandled in every possible way. It seems to have been largely a publicity stunt. The players rejected it as nonsense, when they could have been informed of its value and would then have cooperated.

There is not the slightest doubt that a competent operator, working with a fairly good subject who is a professional baseball player, could increase his seasonal batting average by at least ten percent. In most sports there is a mental hazard present. Whenever this is true, hypnosis could overcome this situation.

Here's a fine example in sports. In 1923 the great Finnish runner Paavo Nurmi astounded the track world by setting a world record for the mile run of 4:10.4. Today many high school runners do better. An English trackman, Roger Bannister, was the first to run under four minutes for this distance. Now scores of others have bettered this time. Coaching methods and training have improved, and running tracks are better, but the main difference has been in the mental attitude of the runners.

As another example, a few years ago a high jumper at

a California university cleared the bar at 6 feet 11 inches or 11½ inches some eighteen times in meets. He was national champion. He never could clear 7 feet. The mental hazard and his expectations were too great. At that time others had cleared this height and now many have done so.

In any game or sport, confidence and expectation are very important. Mental hazards are present in golf, tennis, basketball, football, you name it. Dr. William Kroger of Los Angeles writes in his book *Clinical and Experimental Hypnosis:* "The author has used hypnosis to improve the ability of a considerable number of athletes competing in baseball, football, pugilism and golf, without deleterious effects. The results have ranged from good to spectacular." Kroger also states that hypnotic suggestion increasing the athlete's ability has never been injurious in any way. The athlete is able to exert more of his potential but will never overdo it so he damages himself — again the teleology of the subconscious at work.

Aside from the mental effects possible through hypnosis there is another factor which certainly should interest the athlete, and the coaches. This is entirely physical. In many sports injuries are common, football being the worst example of this. A sprained ankle lays the athlete up for at least ten days. Such a sprain causes much swelling and the ankle is too painful to be used. Actually, using it would be good for it. With hypnosis, athletes with such a sprain have played on the ankle next day, the swelling caused to go down overnight. Hypnotic anesthesia can inhibit the pain of the sprain. Suggestions for rapid healing apparently are very effective, this applying to any wound or injury. Dentists using hypnosis have a great opportunity to observe rapid healing as a result of suggestion.

A woman acquaintance of mine was in a bad automobile accident. Thrown out of the car, she fell so that a femur was driven back through her buttock, out through the skin, and was badly broken. The orthopedic surgeon told her she would be in a plaster cast for six months. After I gave her suggestions of rapid healing, he was able to remove the cast in three months. The surgeon stated that this was incredible.

A few individual athletes have benefited from hypnosis but usually want no publicity about it and do not even tell their fellows about it.

There have been many textbooks written on the clinical aspects of hypnosis. There are many other applications than have been mentioned here, far too many to be even mentioned. Hypnosis has been found useful in migraine, as has been shown, and other chronic headaches, in some skin conditions, in urology, proctology, opthalmology, internal medicine and, in fact, every branch of medicine.

There are other practical applications which have largely been ignored even when called to the attention of authorities. One of these is in the legal sphere, particularly in law enforcement. The courts have held that information or confessions obtained under hypnosis from suspects cannot be used in court cases. This would not prevent the gaining of information and even gaining a confession in some situations.

A Minnesota psychologist who prefers to have no publicity about it, has been called on by police in several cases. One was where a child had been murdered and a prime suspect had been arrested. Hypnotized with indirect induction the psychologist was able to learn from him the location of the body of the child, which had not yet been found. The body was recovered and the suspect then confessed to the crime.

In another case a confession was obtained from a suspect murderer by means of hypnosis. It was tape recorded and later the man repeated his confession without hypnosis being employed, and this could then legally be used in his trial.

In Los Angeles a jewelry store was held up by two

bandits. When they ran out of the store, entered their car and drove away, they passed a young couple on the sidewalk who were passing by. One of the bandits had a gun in his hand which was seen by both of them and they realized a holdup had taken place. When questioned by the police they could only give very vague descriptions of the two bandits and neither could give the license numbers of the car in which they had driven away.

For some reason someone in the police department who knew a bit about hypnosis asked them if they would be willing to be hypnotized and questioned further. Both the man and the girl agreed and the hypnotist was called in. Under hypnosis each gave a thorough description of both criminals and both were able to give the license numbers of the car. They had been interviewed and hypnotized separately. With the car license obtained, the police were able to apprehend and convict the bandits.

It is well-known that witnesses to any event will give wide variances in reporting what they apparently saw. Nevertheless the subconscious will register correctly whatever was witnessed, and this in complete, minute detail. Attorneys familiar with hypnosis, and they certainly are very few, can obtain correct information from witnesses when hypnosis is used.

In the space program it has been hinted that some or all of our astronauts have been taught self-hypnosis and have used it in their space flights. However this seems to be a subject which space authorities deem secret and it is not known if this is true.

Dr. George Estabrooks has done some work with the military, though apparently he has not been able to convince top authorities of the possibilities of hypnosis in connection with brainwashing of captured soldiers by our enemies. Of course one of the brainwashing techniques is by means of hypnosis and also drugs. Estabrooks claims that hypnotic suggestions could set up counters to brainwashing so that it could not be successful. It is very probable that this is true.

Of course no information is obtainable from our CIA, other intelligence organizations, or the military department as to what they may be doing with brainwashing or the interrogation of prisoners. These matters, including the possible uses of hypnosis, are categorized as top secret. It would indeed be strange if these authorities are neglecting to use hypnosis.

In the field of education the applications of self-hypnosis have been described. While it is certain that hypnosis will never be used in the school system because of misinformation and misconceptions about it by both school authorities and by parents, it could well be applied in some situations to school children. Some children do not learn easily which may be due to lack of intelligence or because of emotional difficulties from which the child suffers. Many schools now have programs for emotionally handicapped children, and for those with reading and other problems. Some teachers are specially trained to teach these children. School psychologists interview some of them and give them various psychological tests. Hypnosis could certainly be most helpful in learning what a child's handicapping problems are, and in treating such conditions. Our society is far from ready to have hypnosis used in this way.

24
Hypnosis in Parapsychology

It is obvious that any extrasensory perceptional ability must be a product of the subconscious mind. Can hypnosis be of value then in developing such abilities as telepathy, clairvoyance and precognition?

One of the difficulties in the area of parapsychology is that a great many scientists are afraid of this subject. They will not admit that there is anything factual about it, and are completely closed-minded about it. They resemble the proverbial ostrich, burying their heads in the sand. Of course other scientists are interested in the area and a number of research projects are being carried on in this field. A very few schools now have departments of parapsychology. The leading one was at Duke University, now no longer active. Perhaps the present leader in this field is the University of Virginia.

Strangely enough, the old-time mesmerists often reported the expression of ESP in their subjects, either spontaneously or through suggestion. These reports concerned "traveling" clairvoyance (astral traveling) where the subjects mind could supposedly be sent elsewhere and the subject would report what he presumably saw there. Telepathy was also reported. One interesting report made as to several different subjects was that they could clairvoyantly diagnose disease and recommend its treatment for some patient. This was much the same as was done by the late Edgar Cayce in the twentieth century.

It was claimed by the mesmerists, and also by Pierre Janet using suggestion for induction that hypnosis could be induced at a distance, telepathically. Still another parapsychological faculty reported by some subjects was the ability to feel and report sensations felt by the operator who had hypnotized the subject. For instance the operator might be pinched in various areas and the subject claimed to feel the pinches in the same areas. Also, if the operator tasted various substances, the subject could report experiencing the same taste sensations.

Various attempts have been made to reproduce some of these reported abilities. During the present century none have been successful. The British Society for Psychical Research did some successful experimenting along these lines in the 1880s. Pierre Janet and Charles Richet, a French scientist, had a remarkable subject named Leonie with whom they experimented successfully, and they tried to eliminate any possible fraud. They were able to hypnotize her at a distance of several kilometers. Once when in LeHavre they told her in hypnosis to travel to Richet's laboratory in Paris and report what she saw. Excitedly she exclaimed that it was on fire and burning. This was true and it burned to the ground at that time.

Why have our modern operators failed to reproduce what the old mesmerists claimed? Their reports are not regarded as offering the slightest scientific proof of their claims. No controlled experiments were made. Fraud on the part of some subjects undoubtedly was present. Claims were greatly exaggerated; even false claims were made enthusiastically. Another factor which may be the real answer is that the mesmerists took anywhere from a half hour to four or five hours for their inductions. It seems certain that they produced a much deeper state of hypnosis than is induced by modern operators who rarely take over fifteen or twenty minutes for an induction.

Some modern investigators do report having had successful results. A Swedish psychiatrist, John Jborkhem, conducted extensive research into traveling clairvoyance. He reported that most of the subjects produced nothing but fantasy, and seemed not to have actually visited the places to which they were sent, which was always nearby so checks could be made. However, he found that about two percent of his subjects did astrally travel and reported correctly, under excellent scientific controls. For instance he would have an observer in the next room take a book blindly from a bookcase, open it without looking at it. The subject would then be sent under hypnosis into that room and would be asked the title of the book and the page at which it was opened. Some correct reports were given, though rarely.

Several modern investigators, psychologists and psychiatrists, have conducted experiments in trying to promote telepathy or clairvoyance. Most of these experiments utilized card reading, the calling of cards. Most of these tests have been successful in that the subjects did call the cards better than they would have with chance. The results were significant in that respect, but they were very far from startling.

There have also been experiments in trying to produce hypnotic dreams which would involve target pictures which were enclosed in opaque envelopes. Neither the subjects or the operator knew their contents. The operator would take an envelope, concentrate on it and "will" the subject, in hypnosis, to dream of whatever was in the envelope. There was some success with these tests but, again, nothing remarkable.

The most successful of all modern tests was with a rather remarkable Czechoslovakian subject named Stepnanek. His ESP abilities were developed by a psychologist named Ryzl, now in the United States. Stepanek has been able to determine whether a hidden card was white or green, in thousands of tests. His percentage of correct "guesses" was very far above chance.

All in all modern experiments aimed at developing ESP abilities by means of hypnosis have had very limited success. It is quite possible that we do not know enough about how to bring out such latent abilities. And it is to be suspected that not nearly a deep enough trance is being induced in these experimental subjects.

25
Overcoming Resistance

It is not uncommon for a person to visit a hypnotherapist, willingly pay his fee, then subconsciously fight tooth and nail to keep from becoming hypnotized. What are the reasons for such a situation? There are many possible factors which may be present. The causes may depend on the type of resistance, for there are two kinds, or more properly speaking, two situations which can call for resistance.

The first situation is where there is just resistance to being hypnotized. If this is very strong, probably there will be a complete failure in the induction, to the embarrassment of the operator and the frustration of the subject. Sometimes there is resistance but it is not carried to an extreme and the person does become hypnotized but only enters a light state.

Most reasons for resistance of this type are based on misunderstanding or misconceptions about hypnosis. If the subject feels that induction of hypnosis is to be a battle of wills, he may unconsciously resist merely to prove to himself that his mind is the stronger. Many operators make it a point before attempting inductions to explain the usual misconceptions and to let the prospective subject realize that successful hypnosis is a matter of cooperation and not a contest.

During any induction the skilled operator looks for signs of unconscious resistance. In the standing, counting backward from one hundred, method it was mentioned that resistance is being made if there is difficulty in moving the subject around in a circle. Another sign of resistance is when the subject begins to smile during the induction talk. Sometimes this is only a sign of self-consciousness, but this is a different kind of smile readily apparent. The operator knows that a resisting smile is not directed at him as a person and takes no offense. Sometimes a subject will even laugh in the face of the operator. The wise operator laughs right with him, urges him to continue until the laughter is out of his system.

If a subject is asked to look in the operator's eyes as an eye fixation technique, and the subject's gaze keep turning in some other direction, that, too, is a sign of resistance. Still another sign is when the subject, during the induction talk, develops an itch someplace and reaches to scratch it, this usually being someplace on the face. With the accompanying relaxation as the subject slips into hypnosis, the feeling of lethargy grows. Instead, if the subject moves around, crosses his legs, twists in the chair, those also are signs of resistance. All are done unconsciously as a means of preventing the person from being hypnotized.

What should the operator do when resistance is encountered? He realizes that more time will be needed for success. He will certainly make no tests involving a challenge, for obviously it would not succeed. If the subject is apparently trying to prove that "You can't do this to me. My mind is too strong," he will stop the induction and try to make explanations to end the resistance. He may change the method of induction to something quite different, probably resorting to confusion. This involves talking too rapidly for the subject to follow him, making some statement and a moment later making the opposite statement, contradicting himself. This is not an easy method to master and requires skill but is very effective and the subject slips into hypnosis without realizing it, in order to escape from the confusion.

Depending on the situation, the best way of handling the resistance situation would be to stop the induction and to use the questioning technique to find out the unconscious reasons behind the resistance. A series of questions can usually locate the reason, or reasons.

A very common reason for holding back is fear. And the most common fear is of loss of control. Some people are rigid in self-control and almost invariably are difficult subjects. They will enter a light trance but will not let go enough to reach deeper stages. If the personal relationship between subject and opeator is not a good one, this could cause resistance based on suspicion and fear. Another operator might have excellent results with such a subject.

Another fear which may be involved is the fear that the person might say something while in hypnosis which he would not want known. Of course this never occurs because the subject is fully aware at all times. Explanations can eliminate this fear.

Resistance may be due to unconsciously associating hypnosis to some past experience where the subject was either in hypnosis, perhaps spontaneously, or in some related state. The most common of such associations is to a surgical operation when general anesthesia was used with the patient.

Sometimes an imprint may be acting to prevent the subject from entering hypnosis. A twenty-one-year-old girl visited me and during the first session I undertook an induction but without the least result. She remarked that she was fighting and resisting and could not understand why. This was surprising to me as I had expected to find her an excellent subject. On her next visit questioning with pendulum answers was used to find out the reason for the resistance.

Q.   Is there some fear keeping you from being hypnotized?
A.   No.
Q.   Is there something involved with me as the operator which is causing resistance?
A.   No.
Q.   Is there some past experience to which you are associating?
A.   Yes.
Q.   When did this take place? Was it before you were ten years old?
A.   No.
Q.   Was it before you were fifteen?
A.   No.
Q.   Before eighteen?
A.   Yes.
Q.   Was it when you were fifteen?
A.   No.

Q. When you were sixteen?

A. Yes.

Q. Did this take place at home?

A. Yes.

Q. Was some other person involved?

A. Yes.

Q. Was it a relative?

A. Yes.

Q. Was it a parent?

A. Yes.

Q. Was it your mother?

A. Yes.

Q. Did she say something which has acted as an imprint?

A. Yes.

Q. Is there anything else acting to prevent you from being hypnotized?

A. No.

Susan, as we will call her, now remembered what had happened. She started to laugh. "I know what it was," she said. "I had gone to see an exhibition of hypnosis – a stage show. When the hypnotist asked for volunteers, I went up on the stage together with the girl friend who was with me. I was evidently a very good subject. But when I went home and told my mother she was very upset. She scolded me and told me I must never again let anybody hypnotize me. I guess I've been carrying out her orders!"

When this had been worked out Susan was able to enter a very deep state and there was no further trouble. She was obeying an imprint. The questioning technique can usually be the means of finding the reasons for resistance, but sometimes it fails.

Another way for the operator to proceed is to try to utilize the subject's resistance. This might be by making some suggestion to which the subject must unavoidably respond in some way. For instance, a suggestion could be made like this, "Your right arm, though perhaps it will be the left one instead, is going to develop a feeling of lightness now and may begin to float up toward your face without any volition on your part. Or it might be that instead of getting lighter it will do just the opposite and will begin to feel very heavy, pressing down on the arm of your chair. It may even just remain where it is without the slightest movement. You'll be very observant now as to just which of these alternatives will happen. Will it lift, become heavier and press down, or just remain motionless?"

Whatever happens is a response to the suggestion. Then some other suggestion can be made which involves an unavoidable response.

Aside from reasons for resistance which can be located, no one really knows why one person is a very good subject able to enter the deepest stage of hypnosis, and another person is not hypnotizable at all. There certainly must be reasons for this but it may not be possible to learn the causes. Most children between the ages of six and twelve will quickly enter a deep state. A child can resist, though it is unusual.

A physician who had taken one of our courses believed it would be of advantage to have his two daughters hypnotized so they could have the experience. One was fourteen years old and the other was twelve. Accordingly he made an appointment and brought them to my office. He had given them an explanation of hypnosis and of the usual misconceptions about it.

I asked the younger, Ruth, to come in the inner office, while her sister Margaret and the father waited. A twelve-year-old usually will enter a deep trance very quickly. To my surprise Ruth failed even to become lightly hypnotized. I thought I saw a triumphant expression on her face, but she claimed she was trying to cooperate and could not understand why she resisted. I thought perhaps I knew what was going on, so said nothing and let her return to the waiting room, where she announced that she couldn't be hypnotized.

Taking Margaret next, she proved to be an excellent subject and entered a very deep trance. I showed her how hypnotic anesthesia could be developed, and had her hallucinate a TV program with time distortion. She obviously enjoyed the experience. When we returned to the waiting room she told all about her experiences and was very enthusiastic. I watched Ruth while Margaret was telling of her success and saw her frowning. Suddenly she asked me if I would "try" her again. I agreed.

This time everything was entirely different. Within two minutes she was deeply hypnotized and was able to produce anesthesia and hallucinations just as Margaret had done. On returning to the waiting room she told of her success. Of course the answer was that she had no intention of letting Margaret do something which she could not do. I do not know just why she resisted at first unless it had been because of something Margaret had said before they came, but she simply couldn't continue to let Margaret outdo her.

Adults who are in the old-age category can be good subjects, as has been mentioned, but more usually will only be lightly hypnotized. It is probable that an elderly person is set in his ways and much more rigid than are younger ones.

However, individuals of course will respond in different ways. Motive may be an important factor here.

Most of the reasons for resistance can apply to self-hypnosis as well as when someone else tries to induce the trance. In learning self-hypnosis the questioning method may disclose the causes of resistance and then something can be done to counteract them, enabling the person to reach a deeper state.

Sometimes a person who has only been lightly hypnotized or has been unable to even reach a light state will comment and will say that he tried very hard. For some reason trying is not successful. The subject must relax and let hypnosis come. Many times in this situation where the subject is doubtful or skeptical, the old bugaboo, the Law of Reversed Effect, is working and then the harder the subject tries, the less he is able to be hypnotized. Avoid trying, whether with self-hypnosis or when you are acting as the subject for some operator. It should be remembered, too, that the word *try* implies failure. When you say "I'll try" you really mean you doubt if you'll succeed.

The other type of resistance is concerned with resistance to therapy or whatever purpose of application is to be made with hypnosis. This may involve a resistance to being hypnotized on the basis that through hypnosis the operator might take away a symptom or condition which is greatly needed. In other words the subconscious part of the mind doesn't want its applecart upset. In a therapeutic situation it may be well for the operator to explain that hypnosis is not to be used to take away a needed condition but, by means of hypnosis, insight into the reasons for it may be gained. With an understanding of the condition, it would then become unnecessary and would be lost.

Sometimes a subject may be able to reach a fairly deep state of hypnosis but the condition is not corrected or eliminated. This can apply in self-hypnosis also. Various causes for a condition may make it a needed one. For instance, self-punishment may be a reason. A condition may be, and often is, serving as a defense of some kind. Of course neither the therapist, nor the patient, wants the subconscious to be robbed of a needed defense. In the case of self-punishment, the reasons for feelings of guilt should be explored.

Another reason for this type of resistance can be some past experience which may have been very frightening or unpleasant in some way. We tend to bury unpleasant things, to repress them. We do not want to consciously think of them or remember them. But they can fester in the subconscious and cause complications with their source unrecognized.

When trying to uncover such an experience the patient's inner mind may balk and be unwilling to bring it into consciousness. Some deeply buried memory may be so unpleasant or so traumatic that the resistance cannot be overcome. This can be true with self-hypnosis or when consulting a competent psychotherapist who uses hypnosis.

When such blocking occurs a technique which sometimes is effective is time distortion — having the subject's subconscious regress to the experience and view it with the person's adult, present viewpoint and knowledge. It is suggested that the subconscious is to go back and review this experience in full detail, and it is to do this in just fifteen seconds from the time some signal, such as the word *begin,* is given. Questioning would have determined that there is such an experience affecting the subject. Questioning may have revealed more details about the experience: when it happened, who was present and perhaps other details such as what kind of experience it was. The subconscious should review this at least three times. Then, with the questioning, it should be asked if it was reviewed. If the answer is affirmative, this means the event can now be brought to consciousness. Such a subconscious review may have made it accessible. If not ask if, with better understanding, the person can now be free of the effects. This can be true, but sometimes the resistance is too strong and the inner mind will not even regress to the event.

When being regressed, or if using self-hypnosis and regressing yourself, it is always best to go through the event at least three times and then question to see if that is sufficient to erase it or erase its effects. If not, go through it once or twice more and then repeat the question. The purpose in the regression is not only to gain insight but also to work off the emotions with which the event is charged. Technically, this is called a *catharsis*. The working off of the emotions, their discharge, is an *abreaction*.

Always before a regression is made, questioning should determine whether it is all right for the person to go back to the experience. If too frightening, it might be overwhelming to bring out. With self-hypnosis it is unlikely that you could regress to a great traumatic experience, but you play safe with the questioning. Thus you would never find yourself in some experience which could be overwhelming.

As a case which is an example of resistance and of using a subconscious review of an unpleasant event, a young man named Tom visited me. His condition is called nystagamus. His eyeballs continually moved back and forth sideways, dancing. Ophthalmologists had been unable to clear this up. Tom proved to be a good subject but resistances were encountered when regression was attempted. Questioning had brought out that his eye condition was related to two past experiences, one at eighteen months of age, the other at two years. They had happened at home. Someone else was involved but I could not learn who it was.

Since he would not regress to either experience at a conscious level, his subconscious was told to review the first one, taking fifteen seconds to do so. He then drew himself up into a crouching position in the chair and began to whimper like a child. He kept turning his head to one side and his eyeballs were moving, although the eyelids were closed. He was led through the experience three times and then, with finger signals, was asked if he could bring this into consciousness. The answer was negative. Time did not allow further procedure. He was awakened and asked what had come into his mind during this time. He said he had thought of nothing but had been very frightened, almost in a panic.

At his next session, this technique was repeated. His behavior was the same. After a second time he was able to regress at a conscious level. He told of finding himself lying in a crib, crying. His father entered, very drunk. The father was an alcoholic, he told me. Tom merely cried harder and his father slapped him hard across the eyes.

The second experience, a few months later, was almost a repetition of the first one. His father again slapped him on the face. His nystagamus was an attempt to watch his father and to avoid him, glancing continually from side to side. In this case a subconscious review was sufficient to overcome the resistance and then be able to bring the event into consciousness and thus learn the cause of the condition.

Sometimes when resistance is encountered and the reason cannot be located by other means, it can be suggested that the subject will have a very vivid dream that night, or even during the hypnotic session, which will have to do with the reason for the resistance.

There are some other ways of overcoming resistances, but they are not applicable with self-hypnosis.

Some progress in treating some condition is blocked and there is no progress. This may occur when undergoing therapy or with self-hypnosis. The procedure is the same in either situation. The questioning technique is used to locate the block. This might be because there is still great need for the symptom or condition. It is more likely to occur because an imprint is working. There are several imprinted phrases which can completely block any progress.

A young woman who had been rid of a handicapping condition made an appointment for her mother to have treatment. The middle-aged mother came a little early and I heard her in the waiting-room engaging in fits of coughing. During her interview she explained that there really was not much point in seeing me as she had had this cough ever since she could remember and no treatment had ever ended it.

She proved to be a good subject and with finger replies to questions it was discovered that the cough was psychologically caused and had begun when she was four years old. Here was the questioning as it was continued:

Q.   Did this have to do with an illness of some kind?
A.   Yes.
Q.   Was something said, an imprint set up, which caused the coughing to persist?
A.   Yes.

Q.   Was this something said by your mother?
A.   No.
Q.   By your father?
A.   No.
Q.   Could it have been said by the doctor?
A.   Yes.
Q.   Were you coughing because of the illness?
A.   Yes.

The patient now remembered that she had had whooping cough when she was four years old. Regressed to that time she told of being very ill and of almost dying. Thinking this would occur, the physician had said to the parent in her presence, "She'll never get over this," meaning that she would die.

It was now pointed out to her that she had recovered from the illness. She had not died, but with its literalness, her inner mind had retained the main symptom of the illness, the cough. She had now been coughing for forty years. Another question was then asked: now that she saw the reason for the cough and why she had retained it, could it now be lost? The answer was affirmative and in checking several weeks later, it had not returned. It should be added that as soon as she was hypnotized she had stopped coughing.

There are some similar phrases which if imprinted will also serve to maintain a condition. "Nothing does any good," is one. "What's the use?" is another. These have been mentioned as important, together with probably the worst one, "You'll have to learn to live with this."

Conclusion

From what has been discussed in these chapters it is obvious that hypnosis has a great many values and applications. While many physicians, psychologists, psychiatrists and dentists know little or nothing about it, prejudices in these professions have been greatly modified during the last twenty years. Now hypnosis, for the first time in its history, is a procedure which is acceptable to these professions.

Almost any city, including the smaller ones, and even many smaller towns, will have some professional man who uses hypnosis. In almost every situation where use of hypnosis seems indicated it is much better to seek professional help. A local medical or dental association might be able to suggest a local practitioner.

When it is difficult or impossible to obtain professional help with hypnosis, it often is feasible to use self-help, self-hypnosis. Contraindications have been mentioned. Results will largely depend on the causes for any condition, and as to how superficial they may be. If they are deep-seated, if there are repressions and resistances which are not readily overcome, self-help may be unsuccessful. Many times it does bring excellent results. With some conditions, some psychosomatic illnesses, medical treatment in addition to your own treatment may be needed. In many situations treatment should not be attempted except with some supervision by a physician, particularly in having a correct diagnosis made.

It should also be remembered that hypnosis is no panacea. Even the best qualified practitioner has failures. We do not, as yet, know enough about diseases, about the mind itself, to always succeed. It might be well to remember that in the field of medicine great strides have been made in the prevention of disease, but with the exception of infections alleviated with antibiotics, there are few illnesses which medical treatment can always cure. Drugs very seldomly work on the causes of a condition. They may stifle a symptom or relieve it, as aspirin does with a headache, but they do not treat the causes. Hypnosis, with the methods which have been described here, can deal directly with causes, and is particularly effective in influencing the subconscious part of the mind.

Until something has been learned in some way about hypnosis many people still entertain fears about it. Despite its use for two hundred years, misconceptions which lead to fears are common and widely held. Within the past twenty years tens of thousands of women have gone through childbirth while in hypnosis. Far more people have been treated with hypnotherapy. Many of these people have expressed their satisfaction to others, and have dispelled some of the usual false ideas about hypnosis. Where it was not at all unusual twenty years ago to have a patient refuse hypnotic treatment, now this is a very rare occurence, according to physicians.

With the information given here you now have a proper knowledge of hypnosis and what it can accomplish. Perhaps there will never be any occasion for its use with you, but it can be available to you if necessary.

It should be realized that the cases which have been cited here were such that resistances and repressions were not encountered. Results came within a very short time, perhaps in only one or two sessions. This is exceptional. With many patients the therapist will require a number of visits. Nevertheless hypnotherapy is very brief compared to orthodox methods. With self-hypnosis results will sometimes be seen very quickly, but at other times a number of sessions are needed, and patience is required.

Books for Further Reading

August, Ralph V. *Hypnosis in Obstetrics.* New York, McGraw-Hill.

Elliott, Chandler H. *The Effective Student, a Constructive Method of Study.* New York, Harper & Row.

Elman, Dave. *Explorations in Hypnosis.* Los Angeles, Nash Publishing.

Hook, Julius N. *How to Take Examinations in College.* New York, Barnes & Noble.

Kroger, William S. *Clinical and Experimental Hypnosis.* Philadelphia, Lippincott.

Schaill, William S. *Seven Days to Faster Reading.* North Hollywood, Calif., Wilshire Book Company.

Shaw, S. Irwin. *Clinical Applications of Hypnosis in Dentistry.* Philadelphia, W.B. Saunders Company.

My own books are listed at the front of this volume. In addition, a record by me is available:

End the Cigarette Habit with Self-Hypnosis. Englewood Cliffs, N.J., Folkways-Scholastic Records.

One side is an induction talk. The other side is to help the listener quit smoking.